Rainer Maria Rilke: VISIONS of CHRIST

A Posthumous Cycle of Poems

Rainer Maria Rilke (Woodcut).

Rainer Maria Rilke: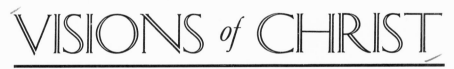

A Posthumous Cycle of Poems

edited, with an introduction, by Siegfried Mandel
poems translated by Aaron Kramer

University of Colorado Press/ Boulder

To
Gunnar Boklund
and
Louie May Miner

Acknowledgments

Appreciation is expressed for permission granted by the Insel-Verlag of Frankfurt am Main, publishers *of Rainer Maria Rilke: Sämtliche Werke,* to translate for the first time Rilke's *Christus-Visionen* and to reproduce the German text from volume III, 1959, of the collected works.

Of especial value have been the poem datings and original manuscript information provided by Ernst Zinn, editor of the *Sämtliche Werke.* Zinn points to extant manuscript title pages from the year 1898, which contain the title *Christus* and the order of seven poems in the first series. In Rilke's diaries and correspondence the poems, however, are referred to mainly as *Christus-Visionen* (*Visions of Christ*). During 1897 and 1898 Rilke noted that five of the poems were completed and ready for publication, the others still had no publishers, and that the rest of the cycle still was to be finished, leaving us with an unclear picture as to the completeness of the cycle. We may accept Zinn's conclusion that "the cycle is not complete but, at the same time, not fragmentary." Zinn's order of seven poems in the first series of the cycle follows Rilke's manuscript pages: "Die Waise," "Der Narr," "Die Kinder," "Der Maler," "Jahrmarkt," "Die Nacht," "Venedig;" "Judenfriedhof" is added. The order followed by Zinn is mentioned so that readers are aware that we instead chose to present the poems in the Rilke cycle in order of their composition, paralled by discussion in the essay.

In speaking of Rilke's posthumous works, Zinn notes: "It is with certainty that only the *Visions of Christ* permit themselves properly to be included in the core of Rilke's own favorite works, and in any case also the collection *In Your Honor"* [the surviving poems written for Lou Andreas-Salomé]. Not only does Zinn see the importance of such early works for the biography of Rilke's poetry but he feels that they represent more than just preparatory stages: "to the attentive eye, decisive traits and penetrating renditions also are evident here."

Rilke, at various points of his life, wrestled with the problems of translating poems from the Russian, Italian, French, and English, and he had the opportunity of evaluating translations made of several of his own poems for an English anthology. He seemed to prefer the words *Nachdichtung* (imitation or copying of another's poetry) and *übertragen* (transposed) to the term Übersetzung (literal translation). A translation is successful *Nachdichtung* or *Übertragung* if it captures the tone, imagery, rhyme, and rhythm of the original, favoring approximation to literalness when necessary.

These guidelines were followed by Aaron Kramer in translating the *Visions* and by Siegfried Mandel in studying each draft in turn, until both were satisfied that a fair representation of the original had been achieved. The virtuosity of Rilke's poetizing made the task of transposition challenging but immensely rewarding if only for the act of re-experiencing the creative form of the original poetry.

We would like to thank the following: the publisher Jos. A. Kienreich, Graz, Austria, for permission to reproduce the photo of Sophia Rilke from her book *Ephemeriden*; the Münchner Stadtmuseum for the photo Oktoberfestwiese; photographer Karl Plicka and ARTIA for *Tombstone of Rabbi Löw* from the book *Prague, the Golden City*.

For the frontispiece woodcut and the line drawing of Rilke, we are grateful to Dorothy Mandel. Our appreciation also is extended to J. K. Emery, Director of Publications at the University of Colorado, for originating the design of the book and seeing it through all stages of production.

For encouragement and suggestions, we are grateful to Dr. Harvey Gross of the University of California at Irvine.

SIEGFRIED MANDEL
AARON KRAMER

Contents

Rainer Maria Rilke: VISIONS of CHRIST

1896 - 1898

Introductory Essay

*I*N the life of every great artist is a watershed where creative energies are channeled away from the juvenile and begin to flow in mature directions. Often the period of emancipation and the efforts to achieve an autonomy of personality and spirit are painful; but when an artist's early upbringing is saturated with piety—as in the life of such significant modern literary pacesetters as Rainer Maria Rilke (1875-1926), Gerhart Hauptmann, and Eugene O'Neill, his complicated personal experience must find an outlet, if not resolution, in his writings. Evidences of clarifying tumultuous ideas and of sifting autobiographical scenes, attempts to formulate concepts, and technical experimentations in the harness of talent are apparent in Rilke's *Visions of Christ* (*Christus: Elf Visionen*) which were written between October 1896 and July 1898 by the poet in his early twenties and in his most critical stage of artistic formation. Because the link between Rilke's biography and poetry is absolute, a study of their relationship throws light upon the *Visions.*

When Rilke returned to his native city of Prague in 1907, eleven years after he had taken flight, he came as a celebrity to give a series of poetry readings; his general impressions were less than enthusiastic:

> Prague itself was confused. Everyone wanted to have me, as though I were edible, —but once they had me, I found them not hungry and as if they had to diet. . . . The reading dull; again the awful old ladies, whom as a child I used to marvel at, and no more amusing now that the marvelling was on their side. A few littérateurs, also the same, dustier, shabbier, and more worn-out with every year, inquisitive and too kind-hearted and too easygoing to be envious.[1]

These judgments—subjective and retrospective—clearly are in justification of his earlier decision to loosen the grip of Prague and escape dilettantism. Franz Kafka, unlike Rilke and Franz Werfel, left too late, regretfully saying, "Prague will not let go. . . . This little motherkin has claws. So one must either conform or. . . ." Traditions of family and milieu forced the young either to conform or to rebel, and at times to create a tormented literature. Although Kafka's macabre novels and short stories are best known of the Prague group of writers, Rilke's tales and those of Gustav Meyrink, Leo Perutz, and Max Brod also abound with mystagogy, occultism, morbidity, neurasthenic eroticism, or pietistic ecstasy.

[1]Letter to Clara Rilke, November 4, 1907.

3

Prague was not only the center of Bohemia (Czechoslovakia today), the most westerly of Slavonic lands, but it became also since the ninth century the economic and cultural crossroad for the Roman West and the Byzantine East, the meeting place of diverse liturgies and languages, the scene of indigenous and foreign peoples, the locale where Romanesque Gothic, Renaissance and Baroque mansions, religious statuary, cathedrals, churches, castles, cemeteries, and monasteries proliferated. It was a city whose various old and older quarters were accessible by stone bridges over the Vltava. And outside of the city was the Bohemian countryside as Rilke knew it and described it during a hard glazed autumn afternoon,

4

> hilly like light music and all at once level again behind its apple trees, flat without much horizon and divided up through the plowed fields and rows of trees like a folk song from refrain to refrain.[2]

Rilke celebrated these country scenes and city sights in several pamphlet-volumes of poetry—between 1895 and 1897—redolent with romantic vagaries as well as sharp impressions. The remote past lived in the present, in ruins, in legends; the historical past— symbolized by the martyred John Huss, Kaiser Rudolph, Saint Wenceslas, the wise Rabbi Löw, the seventeenth century soldiery of the Thirty Years War—still lived in monuments and markers. The immediate time held residues of the 1848-49 revolutions and unresolved Czech nationalist aspirations and struggles against Austro-Hungarian domination. How well this mélange of visual, literary, and historical traditions was

assimilated by the young Rilke may be gauged by his first works and later retrospective flashes.

However rich the sources were for creative activity, they at the same time served to alienate Rilke and other young non-Czech writers from their own economically and politically favored families. They were neither at home in the tiny, restrictive bourgeois-enclave of Austrian or German oriented society—which they detested, nor could they completely identify with the socio-nationalistic elements of the Czech. The bilingual life of Prague had an impoverishing rather than an enriching effect upon the German language which was watered into abstractness and a mixture called "Kuchelböhmisch." The unholy contact of the antagonistic Czech and German language bodies, as Rilke described it later from a distance, deteriorated the edges of language; "whoever was brought up in Prague," wrote Rilke self-consciously, "was entertained from his earliest with corrupted linguistic practices so that later one developed inevitably a disinclination, even a sense of shame, toward things immediate and tender."[3] The imitation of naturalistic dramas rife in Germany—with their fairly coarse idiom and dialects—did not help matters. Ultimately the German writers in Prague had no

[2]Rilke's hymns to the Bohemian countryside and to Prague are pronounced in the early poetry. The quote here from a letter to Clara Rilke, November 4, 1907, may be compared with the long essay *Böhmische Schlendertage*, SW V, pp. 287-300. The distance of years did not change Rilke's affectionate memories of scenes tinged with antiquity.

[3]To the literary historian, philologist, and an early academic mentor August Sauer, January 11, 1914.

greater audience than the set of intellectuals who frequented the coffee houses.

As if these circumstances were not sufficient liabilities, one must add to them certain biographical elements. From the earliest, young René—a name given him through Catholic baptism in 1875—was a tug-of-war object between his father Joseph who envisioned his son as a future solid burgher and his mother Sophia (Phia) who dreamed of shaping a poet laureate. Neither parent was happy. Joseph had to settle for a position with the railroad, obtained for him by his newly-titled brother Jaroslav, Ritter Rilke von Rüliken—married to a baroness and a deputy in Bohemia's assembly. After ten years Joseph Rilke's military career was aborted by illness. Sophia, on the other hand, had to settle for far less than the life of exciting high society to which the vivacious girl had been accustomed in her parental mansion. Both were captive creatures of extreme vanity. Habitually Sophia would walk her son to the Piaristen, an upper class grade school, making certain that René would keep his distance from the Czech children. Shortly before René entered the academy at St. Pölten in 1885, his parents parted ways and the boy was deeply scarred. In later years Rilke loved to characterize his five years at the academy as years spent in a House of the Dead, but we know from other sources that he was permitted to recite his poetry and had the respect of some students and teachers. His mother's overwrought letters may have been the goads that impelled him to seek the nearby graveyard for solitude and poetizing. In the Militärober-realschule at Mährich-Weisskirchen, he lasted from September 1890 to July 1891, being furloughed permanently because of illness. Like his father he was not destined for a military career. His disappointed relatives sent him to a business school in Linz, an "asylum" for academic and military failures. What he neglected in studies, he more than made up for by a "silly escapade" with an instructress. This extra-curricular affair may have had much to do with a sunnier outlook upon life but it resulted in his being pulled back to Prague and being quartered in the apartment of an old aunt. By this time, René had begun to feel that his fate was to live in "comfortable, penurious dependency—like a child of thieves."[1]

During the personally hectic years from 1892 to 1896, Rilke led a dual life. Long, hard work with private tutors went into his studies of religion, philosophy, and German language for school examinations, matriculations at the Gymnasium, and then auditing at the German branch of Prague's Karl-Ferdinand Universität—meeting with the approval of his relatives; later his attitude became indifferent toward the academic. Equally energetic was his life among the literati. He hungered after fame and sought it by publishing poems—prolific, uneven, and often imitative; short stories in which the mother figure played a sinister and possessive role; imitative dramas—soon

5

[1]Many letters indicate that René felt himself to be a burden upon family and relatives and that they wished to channel his life into professional and conventional directions. His rebellion against their localisms and vocational objectives is most strongly expressed in a letter to Ludwig Ganghofer, April 16, 1897.

performed to friendly applause and soon forgotten—in the dreariest vein of naturalistic hopelessness and with bitter recrimination against human exploitation and domestic incompatibilities; and a stream of articles, theatre and book reviews, and even an opera-libretto.[5] The German theatre in Prague was hospitable to an odd assortment of fare from the popular to the serious. Plays by Ibsen, Gerhart Hauptmann, and Arthur Schnitzler and Wagner's and Verdi's operas were performed, as well as Shakespeare's *Timon of Athens*. The arts were not completely dead; but even at their weakest, the theatrical importations contrasted starkly with the dearth of local achievement. What Rilke lacked at the time was exposure to Baudelaire, Verlaine, and Mallarmé. (Stefan George had learned much from Mallarmé before returning to Germany to become a force in poetic circles.) Only later was Rilke to acquaint himself with their works —the effects were to be profound.

The self-stylization of Rilke as a gallant may have been encouraged by his years of companionship with Valéry von David-Rhonfeld, who was several years older than René. She subsidized the printing of his first poetic efforts and showered him with admiration that turned to spite when he cast her off; yet, Valéry had given him his first taste of freedom. More ambitious fantasies were pursued when he characterized himself as a court poet—another Torquato Tasso—in the service of the Baroness Láska van Oestéren whose castle he stormed almost literally, or when he devotedly and vainly dogged the steps of a young actress Jenka Carsen.

Despite the congenial comradeship which René found in a number of writer cliques, his ambitions were more cosmopolitan. When the collaborative literary journal *Wegwarten* (*Wild Chicory*) was discontinued after three issues, and when plans failed in 1896 for an editorship of an Austrian edition of the bi-monthly periodical *Jung-Deutschland und Jung Elsass* to which he had been contributing, his disillusionment with attempts to broaden in any significant way the cultural base of Prague was complete. Yet when his chosen literary idol the poet Detlev von Liliencron responded to idolatry with letters of salute, "My glorious René Maria," the young man's self-confidence and ego ballooned again; he tried to impress people with the esteem of the older poet. Already he had made contact with personages and publishers outside of Prague and tried to solidify his acquaintanceships with quick, restless trips to Budapest, Vienna, and Swiss Bohemia. Especially rewarding were his visits to the notable art galleries in Dresden. Impatiently he wanted to put into practice his poetic dictum, "If the time does not create its great men,/ man must create for himself a time of greatness." In preparation, he had a group of poems ready under the title of *Crowned with Dreams* (*Traumgekrönt*). Several cities beckoned with their live cultural centers and publishers: Vienna (which was ruled out primarily because his mother was there), Berlin, Hamburg,

---

[5]Rilke's short plays *Im Frühfrost* (*Hoar Frost*) and *Jetzt und in der Stunde unseres Absterbens* (*Now and in the Hour of our Dying*) were performed in Prague in 1896 and 1897. In these unsuccessful plays, the influences of Gerhart Hauptmann and others of the school of naturalism are evident.

Munich. Even in these places little that was notable literature materialized until about 1911; France, England, and Russia were far ahead. For his new environment, Rilke chose Munich probably because of his publishing outlets there and the friendly reception he had received in the circle of the popular writer Ludwig Ganghofer. To Ganghofer he was to write,

> With every day it becomes clearer to me that I was right in setting myself from the start against the phrase my relatives like: Art is something one just cultivates on the side in one's free hours, when one leaves the government office. . . That to me is a fearful sentence. I feel that this is my belief: Whoever does not consecrate himself wholly to art with all its wishes and values can never reach the highest goal. He is not an artist at all. And now it can be no presumption if I confess myself to be an artist, weak and wavering in strength and boldness, yet aware of bright goals, and hence to me every creative activity is serious, glorious, and true. Not as martyrdom do I regard art—but as a battle the chosen one has to wage with himself and his environment in order to go forward with a pure heart to the greatest goal. . . But this needs a whole man! Not a few weary leisure hours.[6]

In the phraseology of "consecration" to art and the idea of the artist as a "chosen one," we find the fledgling poet shaping his art into a form of religion.

The environment struggles which Rilke talks about can be illustrated by three scenes from his autobiographical novella *Ewald Tragy* (written in 1898 and published posthumously) which depicts his last days in Prague. When the young man tells his father of his intentions of going to work in Munich, the Herr Inspektor of the story, seeing no need for the footloose adventure, lectures his son: "You have your

room, your food . . . and if you treat people correctly, the finest homes are open to you." With scorn the poet answers that all his father's world consists of is money and people and the necessity of being abject to both. With icy detachment and satire, Rilke pays back the disparagement of his poetizing by his class-conscious and titled relatives when he dramatizes a family banquet, a brittle salon concert guided by the ridiculous tinkle of a piano, and a contest in imitation of animal voices that deteriorates into a series of cackles and shrieks; he regards the familial ensemble as the living dead, much as Joyce was to view some of his Dubliners. More revealing is a scene between the poet and his old aunt. With bohemian playfulness he says, "I am my own law-giver and king; above me is no one, not even God." The aunt cries and tells the poet that insane asylums and corrective institutions exist to accommodate his type. The poet becomes hysterical, "No . . . There is no one like me, there has never been anyone like me." After he regains his composure he is deeply embarrassed at having revealed his inmost secret. Quite clearly Rilke's egotistic display was a sign of the young poet defining his goals and then striving to live up to them.

7

* * *

With Rilke's move from Prague to Munich in September 1896 came a period of contemplation, a summing up of experience, and a firmer sense of direction. The first poetic task which engaged his attention in Munich was a cycle of poems which he

[6]Letter, April 16, 1897.

A caricature of Rilke during his Prague
days by a friend, Emil Orlik, 1896.

referred to in correspondence and conversation as *Visionen* (*Visions*) or more frequently *Christusvisionen* (*Visions of Christ* or *Christ Visions*). If it seems strange that Rilke wanted to launch his new poetry cycle from so esoteric a base, one must understand that Rilke was reshaping his ideology under the impact of highly personal experiences and general currents of thought. The first engages our close attention while the latter may be sketched briefly.

By Rilke's time, the nineteenth century spirit of *laissez-faire* had drastically changed men's orientation. What the historian J. A. Froude said of England in the 1840's also characterizes subsequent developments throughout Europe: "It was an era of new ideas, of swift if silent spiritual revolution." In time the revolution, abetted by Darwinian and Marxian ideas, gained momentum. Of prime significance was the rending away of the Church from its old anchorage while materialism and skepticism had pervasive effects. Religious controversy and the "higher criticism" particularly helped to erode Biblical infallibility and the Tractarians and Christologists closely reevaluated dogma and problems of historicity.[7] In the forefront of controversy were such books as the theologian David Friedrich Strauss' *Das Leben Jesu* (1835/36; translated into English by George Eliot in 1846 as *The Life of Jesus*), viewing Jesus as a human about whose life myths were woven; Ludwig Feuerbach's *Das Wesen der Religion* (1851) (*The Essence of Religion*), suggesting that the hereafter is nothing but the present idealized, that theology is the product of the human spirit, and that the concept of God is an

ideal rationalized and projected from the best instincts of man; Ernest Renan's *La vie de Jésus* (1863) —an antidote to the defensive and romantic *Le Genie du Christianisme* (1802) by François de Chateaubriand— and J. R. Seeley's *Ecce Homo* (1865), portraying Jesus in human dimensions, without recourse to metaphysics. The fray was joined by scientists who pointed to biological and zoological findings incompatible with the Bible, and by materialists who saw man as a product not of spiritual but of environmental forces and those of his immediate milieu, although some like Pasteur stoutly maintained orthodox belief. Some skeptics accepted the higher criticism and the implications of new teachings of science but were unwilling to proclaim these views publicly lest the structure of society be threatened or out of fear of becoming embroiled in controversy. Rilke was to be in a similar situation with his *Visions*.

Artists and writers were not unaffected by the controversies and took a "notoriously" individualistic view of religious themes. In protest against what he felt to be an encroachment by art upon religion, a gentleman by the name of T. Chambers arose in the House of Commons in 1869 to declare: "while a community might and ought to be preached at and lectured by the Philosopher and the minister of religion

9

[7]How deeply the English intellectuals of the Victorian period felt that they lived in a "marked" time, a time when religion and the church had to undergo changes, may be seen in two excellent studies: J. H. Buckley, *The Victorian Temper*, New York: Knopf, 1964; W. L. Burn, *The Age of Equipoise: A Study of the Mid-Victorian Generation*, New York: Norton, 1964.

it was not for the artist to take upon him that duty."[8] In addition to the inclination toward preaching, the artist's transvaluation of religion in the 19th century was most strongly influenced by Thomas Carlyle's dictum: the poet-artist is the superior priest; his works of Beauty include and transcend Truth. Carlyle exalted the beautiful over the good and the artist as morally superior to the prophet and Matthew Arnold predicted that poetry would replace religion. Echoes of such enunciations were soon heard from Pater, Whistler, Wilde, and Yeats. Similar chords were struck in Germany as Friedrich Schlegel proclaimed, "Only he is an artist who has religion of his own, an original view of infinity." Even more drastic were Richard Wagner's dreams to make art a religion and the opera house its temple. And with Wagnerian prose and rhapsodic sermons Nietzsche poured scorn upon the anti-intellectualism of mass thought and the un-Christian aspects of the religion-professing times. In a gentler vein, Ralph Waldo Emerson (the subject of a Rilke lecture) exhorted the "dead alive" mass man to listen to "the voice of God in the intuition of the heart"; like the Antinomians and other Puritan "heretics," he asserted a private faith. "The poet," wrote Emerson, "is the sayer, the namer . . . a sovereign . . . emperor in his own right." Most brilliant in 19th century literature in this regard is Dostoevsky's Grand Inquisitor scene in *The Brothers Karamazov* which raises the subject of how little remains in the modern world of Christ's ancient teachings. The theological experience is variously conceived and expressed also by such 19th century writers as De Quincy,

Robert Browning, Emily Bronte, Arnold, Hopkins, Swinburne, Hawthorne, Emily Dickinson.[9] In the works of Lamartine, Vigny, Hugo, and Musset, the figure of Christ became a symbolic synonym for the modern poet—a humanitarian guide, a forsaken and lonely prophet who—with unintentional irony—preaches fruitlessly.[10]

In short, theologians, philosophers, and an inexhaustible array of literary personages touched upon, in one way or another, major religious issues and reinterpreted the savior-archetype figure of Christ. One critic has evaluated the phenomenon in this fashion: "It is as natural for the Western writer of tragedy to make Christ his objective correlative, against which he measures the experience of man, as it was for the Greek playwright to build his tragedy around the stories of Dionysus. Both figures are topical dramatizations of the archetype of the sacrificial hero."[11]

[8]Burn, p. 280, fn.

[9]These figures are discussed in their orientation to religion by J. Hillis Miller, *The Disappearance of God*, Cambridge: Harvard University Press, 1963.

[10]Judging the French romanticists by Catholic criteria, a dim view is taken by Mother Maria Consolata, *Christ in the Poetry of Lamartine, Vigny, Hugo, and Musset* (doctoral dissertation, Bryn Mawr, 1947). The study affords a close look at the poets' interpretation of Christ.

[11]E. M. Moseley, *Pseudonyms of Christ in the Modern Novel: Motifs and Methods*, Pittsburgh: University of Pittsburgh Press, 1962, p. 24. Whether central or peripheral, the preoccupation with Christ by modern writers is impressive as shown by Moseley's study of Conrad, Dostoevsky, Turgenev, Lawrence, Remarque, Fitzgerald, Faulkner, Forster, Steinbeck, Silone, Malraux, Koestler, Camus and Hemingway.

However, one can note as well some other historical shifts of emphasis. One common idea, despite the diversities of ritual and philosophy, that seemed dominant among the ancients was the need for a mediator between man and God as represented by the figures of Prometheus, Dionysus, Mithras, Moses, Christ; during the Middle Ages especially, Mary and the saints were venerated as intercessors. With the impact of the Reformation and the influence of the mystics, a closer man-God relationship became envisioned and evident. Some philosophers and writers by emphasizing the man-God relationship de-emphasized the Christ figure; others scaled Christ to human dimensions, eliminating him as an intercessor, rejecting the Pauline interpretations, and accepting the views of the communal primitive church. With some reservations, Rilke was inclined toward interpretations favoring Christ not as divine but as human.

Some of the intellectual currents which I have sketched touched Rilke. To those must be added his reading of Goethe—though sparse, Heine (especially the polemics), Nietzsche, and Rilke's academic studies in religion and philosophy. Direct discussion of contemporary religious issues occurred during his Prague "castle" days when he collaborated with the Baroness Láska's brother Friedrich Werner van Oestéren on one of the issues of the *Wegwarten* periodical. Friedrich was to receive attention for his contributions to German-Bohemian literature and particularly for his political novel *Christus nicht Jesus* (*Christ, not Jesus*), taken from his educational experience at a Jesuit seminary. The title of course draws distinction between

Christ as the Greek-derived form of *Christos*, the Messiah, and Jesus the moralist and teacher; the Jesuits—who emphasized the martyriological aspects of Christ—are portrayed as pursuing worldly rather than idealistic goals.

* * *

Every artist has an outer and an inner biography. The outer biography consists of dates and events as well as the artist's obvious relation to intellectual currents; the inner biography consists of personal insights and the reflections of the inner mind which reacts, sifts, and interprets. Rilke measured the worth of his writings by the necessity out of which they arose, but he reserved for himself the decision of keeping out of print those works which unambiguously revealed his inner biography, most specifically his *Visions of Christ*, the novella *Ewald Tragy*, and many observations recorded in his diaries. The prolific publication of poems, stories, dramas, and articles makes apparent the surface activity during his Prague days, while the long unpublished works mirror the subsurface and those experiences that become lifelong grist for the inner biography. The route to the *Visions* is best taken through experiences and observations which Rilke thought critical in his years of rebellion and esthetic formulations.

The recently published memoir of Frau Hertha Koenig, one of Rilke's many benefactresses, covers some old ground but does it from a new vantage point, namely through a portrait of Rilke's mother. Upon first meeting Sophia Rilke in 1917, Frau Koenig—as

11

related in *Rilkes Mutter*[12]—was able to understand and share the apprehensive feeling which came over Rilke whenever he felt the presence of his mother with her determined voice and restless, searching eyes: "The close ties with her Catholic church were so strongly apparent that one almost felt it indecorous to sit next to this woman in an earthly sphere and to have other than pious thoughts." In 1930, four years after Rilke's death, Frau Koenig on several occasions visited the 79-year old Sophia in Munich. Dressed in stylish mourning, Sophia embodied the paradox between extreme piety and vanity. Consciously she strove for her old elegance in dress and touched up her hair with the black of charred corks; at the same time she decorated a table as if it were an altar—a brass crucifix and burning candles flanked a picture of her son and a memorial hour was set aside daily during which she imagined herself to be with her son. Sometimes Sophia would startle a visitor by placing a finger on her lips, with the admonition that God was listening. The crucifix reminded her of things past: "Look here, once I taught René how one must pray—he was three years old—and that great suffering came from the Savior and that therefore we must never complain when we suffer." She also recounted the time when she rushed to the bedside of her "Renetscherl" who sobbed, "But mama, how can I fall asleep, I haven't yet given the dear God a kiss." She gave him the small brass crucifix and calmed him. At other times Sophia would tell Frau Koenig, with great self-satisfaction: "Once I used to be the best dancer, the best skater . . . René was proud of his

elegant Mama, loved it dearly when I dressed well. Others were often so fat but *I* always slim, paying attention to appearances." The commingling and the impact upon the child of the pietistic and the erotic are powerfully drawn in Rilke's novel *Malte Lauride Briggs* and become deeply marked in his poetic works —including the *Visions*, as is the ambivalence of love and hate for the mother figure.[13]

Although Sophia claimed that by her rigorous example she taught René how to pray, she seemed to ignore what his *alter ego* Malte reported in the novel of 1910. Of Mama he wrote, "She did not really teach me how to pray; however, it was soothing to her that I gladly kneeled and that I now clasped my hands and then folded them upright—just as it seemed most expressive for me to do." The youngster very early learned how to dissemble or at best to shape his at-

[12]Hertha Koenig, *Rilkes Mutter*, Tübingen: Neske, 1963. The quotes in my discussion are translated from the 32-page memoir.

[13]Few first-hand sources which give us a picture of Rilke's mother and father are unbiased. Rilke's son-in-law in his *René Rilke: Die Jugend Rainer Maria Rilkes* claimed that Rilke's childhood was not as grim as the poet has limned it, but that his mother's grotesque bigotry, akin to that of converts, did much to unsettle the child who learned to talk of God as "Himmelspapa," Papa in heaven, and of Maria (the Virgin Mary) as "Himmelsmama," Mama in heaven. Sieber gave such a totally unsympathetic and spiteful account of Sophia that it evoked an indignant reply by Wolfgang Schneditz in an introduction to a reissued volume of aphorisms, written by Phia Rilke and originally published in 1900, *Ephemeriden*, Graz: Kienreich, 1949. Schneditz defended Sophia as a courageous and witty woman who tried to maintain the prestige of her family status; he notes that Rilke's heirs have avoided the release of the correspondence between mother and

12

Sophia Rilke (1851-1931)

titude in ways to please his mother. In contrast, the boy's father exhibited "a complete correctness and immaculate courtesy; in church it seemed to me sometimes that he was chief huntsman in God's service." Caught in the cross-current of his parents' disaffection for one another and their contrasting religious miens, the boy was confused. The echo of such scenes reverberate in the *Visions* and in the corridor of Rilke's mind for the rest of his life. He told Frau Koenig in 1917, and many others before her, that his mother with typical willfulness had wished to correct the mistake of fate which had given her a son instead of another girl in place of the one that died. She made him wear long blond locks and stubbornly dressed him like a little girl as long as possible. And, as part of his outfitting for the military school, his mother had given him linen and underclothing with delicate embroidery which exposed him to the ridicule of schoolmates and superiors. One of them tore off a

medallion on a thin chain about his neck. So alive remained the memory, although more than thirty years had passed, that Frau Koenig imagined that Rilke still felt the cut upon retelling the story.

Also indelible in his memory was the childish tormentor who struck him in the face. According to one of Rilke's versions, he reacted by saying, "I suffer it because Christ suffered it, silently and without complaint, and while you were hitting me, I prayed my good God to forgive you." At first the tormentor was struck dumb but then broke into derisive laughter and spread the story; this resulted in more laughter. The young René prayed for death but no response came. In another version, he flew into a towering rage and predicted that the tormentor would be punished; the tormentor promptly fell and broke his leg. Since the first version was told to his betrothed Vally in 1894, while the other came many years later as a retrospective wish fantasy of what should have happened, we

14

son and that this would be indispensable for accurate biography. Of course, one cannot judge until the correspondence becomes public but in one Sieber excerpt and one long letter of Christmas of 1925 (published in 1945), signed with his discarded name René, one sees a devoutness and a son so loving and appreciative that he seems to be a person other than the one who wrote so disparagingly of his mother in his poetry and in letters to numerous friends and acquaintances. Two things, I believe, are at work here. First, Rilke suffered a personal conflict between love and hate. Son and mother alike possessed an indomitable will, a streak of independence, imaginative faculties, supersensitivity or hypochondria, and were prone to mediumistic and supernatural superstitions; Rilke resented his own resemblance to his mother. Second, in the presence of the mother—or in correspondence, the son, as he himself once said, is made to "feel small with her again," experiencing it seems a psychological regression into childhood.

Frau Koenig in her memoirs notes Rilke's timidity and shrinking in the company of his mother. A startling parallel emerges when we compare an account given by a much older second cousin of Rilke who described the little René as a tender and intimidated child ("verschüchtertes Kind") who, during her only visit to the family, constantly clung to his mother's hand. Of Joseph and Sophia Rilke, cousin Anna Grosser-Rilke wrote in her *Nie Verwehte Klänge: Lebenserinnerungen aus acht Jahrzehnten*, Leipzig: Beyer, 1937: "Joseph Rilke cut a stately figure. Rainer Maria's mother, Sophia, lives in my memory as a fantastic woman, a strict Catholic and—I am almost tempted to say—a bit exalted for contemporary tastes. She possessed a firm belief that her son was a God-graced genius. None of the family relatives or close friends shared this opinion and she was ridiculed as a mother with an exaggerated love. But time has proved her to be correct" (p. 15).

can see his early disillusionment with meekness and passivity; they seemed to be inoperative virtues. When the child received no answer to some material prayer his mother would tell him that God was quite busy and that his prayer would have to wait its turn,[14] an answer whose superficiality became painfully apparent when the boy matured. Finally, conventional prayer became synonymous for him with distasteful command as when in the military school the non-commissioned officer would walk down the aisle of beds "as if he were in the service of silence and darkness," "Right-side turn, 'heavenly Father' pray; go to sleep!" From a number of sources, then, came authoritarian intrusions into a sensitive area of the child's psyche, which proved disruptive.

From that time, said Rilke of the military school,

> . . . after long fearful battles, I abandoned the violent Catholic piety of childhood, made myself free of it in order to be even more, even more comfortlessly alone; but from things, from their patient bearing and enduring, a new, greater and more devout love came to me later, some kind of faith that knows no fear and no bounds. In this faith life is also a part.[15]

The faith that knows no bounds was to be found in art, a conviction—like that of Carlyle and Arnold—which grew in the late Prague years. Abandoning the violent piety of which he spoke meant hauling in anchor and temporarily drifting to another extreme. In a poem of 1893, "Glaubensbekenntnis,"[16] "Confession of Faith," he defiantly strikes an atheistic pose, satirizing the congregational sheep who dociley accept the dogma of the Trinity and the sacrifice of Christ for mankind, who reject this life in favor of the next, and who choose a comfortable illusion instead of reality. To the threat that he will be doomed when the trumpet sounds for the resurrection of the dead, he saucily answers, "Have thanks—I'll remain lying/ and be satisfied/ with this the *only* world." Reward, he notes, comes in this world through love, a teaching "which to me is religion."

In another poem also written in 1893—"Christus am Kreuz," "Christ on the Cross," lay the seeds of the later cycle of Visions. Around a modest wooden cross with a garishly colored figure of Christ stand two children immersed in prayer, "Give us this day our daily bread." Choked with sympathy, the poet says, "Who can rob them of their hope, whose budding breaks through their meager life." Prayer has given their work-weary limbs new strength. Almost jealous of their faith and with a doubt-torn heart, he asks himself why he cannot pray and why he sees nothing except a piece of colored metal when he looks at Christ from whom the others sought help. The answer comes to the poet:

> He was, like me, a person,—but he trusted
> far more upon his powers than he should . . .
> That he was great was proved by his devotion
> to noble aims. But one thing made him small:
> that he, in the excess of his emotion,
> denied he was a person like us all . . .
> Precisely at the time his power spread
> across the whole wide earth by every road,

[14]Sieber, p. 170.

[15]Letter to Ellen Key, April 3, 1903.

[16]SW III, pp. 489-91.

precisely then he might have proudly said:
I who accomplished this am flesh and blood!
Within him, though, that lust for homage woke
because of which so many a great man falters,—
he wished that someday for his sake the smoke
would climb into the skies from golden alters.
Not worship as a man did he desire,—
no, he would rather suffer and expire,
die on the cross—but die with a God's name.
It's clear to me now why I neither can
love and adore him, nor unto him call:
he would have stayed so godlike as a man;
as god he seems so human now, so small!"
I looked up, where upon the cross hung grim
the painted figure with averted face.
Day came at last—I turned my back on him
and dried my tears . . . . and then I left the place.[17]

16

The poet's almost colloquial argument was to become a refrain in the *Visions*: Christ as a man possesses godly greatness but as a presumptive divinity seems so humanly small and vain.[18] Rilke's view about Christ and God was prudently kept from family, relatives, and public print. Rilke's view of the deliberateness of Christ's martyrdom in order to help fulfill the Messianic prophecy was not original; Goethe, historians, among others, have theorized in this vein. Christ on the cross has not infrequently caused poets to react literally and to lament the impossibility of faith in so disconsolate a figure. We find a parallel to Rilke's thoughts in the French romanticist Alfred de Musset who in his youth indicated that he would wish for nothing better than to be able to believe, but that reality—"a world too old"—prohibited it. In his poem "Rolla" he pronounces both the cause and the body of Christ to be dead: "Ta gloire est morte, ô Christ! et sur nos croix d'ébène/Ton cadavre céleste en poussière est tombé," (Your glory is dead, oh Christ, and on our cross of ebony/Your heavenly corpse has fallen into dust).

Somber religious themes such as these were rare in Rilke's Prague years as he pursued academic and literary goals as well as life's pleasures and pleasantries. In Munich however, he hoped to chart his way into the "open" and to dedicate himself to the vocation of poetry; he keenly felt the contrast between the rather gay atmosphere of Prague and the serious tasks he had set himself in strange surroundings. Between October 5 and 9, 1896—in the creative smithy which he called "work and solitude," "Arbeit und Einsamkeit," he finished three poems in the *Visions of Christ* cycle.

* * *

All of the eleven Christ poems are narratives in dramatic verse telling of Christ's role as eternal wanderer and his appearance—physical and spiritual—mainly in the modern world. Rilke's technique consists of giving an opening setting, with personal commentary, and then introducing various characters whose

[17]The full German text may be found in SW III, pp. 491-93: translation of the excerpt by Aaron Kramer.

[18]The arguments of this poem are not unfamiliar to poets in rebellion against tradition and in search of personal values. Emily Dickinson wrote, "When Jesus tells us about his Father, we distrust him. When he shows us his Home, we turn away, but when he confides in us that he is 'acquainted with Grief,' we listen, for that is also Acquaintance of our Own" (Letter to Mrs. Henry Hills, c. 1884).

dialogues progress toward a sharp conclusion or implication. Prominent are dialogues between Christ and children protected by their naiveté, a painter, a fallen woman, a magistrate, and God. In most of the scenes Christ is faced with the results of his teachings or rather their distortion by his followers.

In the first of Rilke's fables, he joins the poets and artists who are attracted by the dramatic potentials of orphaned children and Christ's love for children. Despite the simplicity of rendering these themes, as with Wordsworth's "We are Seven," bathos and cloying effects lurk dangerously. Already in a prose sketch *Das Christkind, The Christchild,* written in 1893, the same year as his "Confession of Faith" poem, Rilke captures the hallucinations in the mind of a dying child imbued with the religious teachings of a heaven after the earthly life; there is no trace of irony in the sketch just as there is none in the first poem, "Die Waise," in the *Visions* cycle. Rilke's treatment of the effect of religious indoctrination upon children is based on personal experience with the added knowledge of Gerhart Hauptmann's play *Hanneles Himmelfahrt, Hannele's Ascension,* which Rilke probably saw in Prague several years after its initial performance in 1893 in Germany. From today's vantage point, it is difficult to understand the sensation evoked by so innocuous a play.[19] Audiences and readers were split into warring groups. Sociologists and "naturalists" condemned *Hannele* for its failure to represent real human nature, the devout Protestant Kaiser Wilhelm II of Germany hailed it as "the beginning of a school of Christian drama," his Catholic Majesty of Austria endorsed it, some critics scored its sickly piety, others were appalled by the playwright's naturalistic treatment of a story in which the coarse proletarian parents of Hannele caused her death through cruelty. The New York Society for the Prevention of Cruelty to Children successfully barred a child actress from playing the role of the deranged Hannele who in a fever vision saw Christ; objections were raised to the effects of "awful blasphemy" and "the revolting and horrible travesty of a resurrection." In France, critics praised the play's psychological plausibility. While Hauptmann found himself with an unintentionally controversial play which helped to launch his name, theater managers were primarily concerned with its box office appeal. Hauptmann called his play "Traumdichtung," a dream poem. Rilke was to characterize his *Visions of Christ* as "Traumepen," dream epics, and "epischlyrische Phantasien," epic-lyric fantasies; but in other respects, Rilke's interpretations differed from Hauptmann's. The furor caused at that time by secular treatment of religious matter probably was not lost upon Rilke.

In Rilke's "Die Waise," Christ makes his appearance at a critical point of a little orphan girl's life. She has just come from the second-class funeral of her mother and her mind is shielded by religious indoctrinations that calm her grief. Against the churchyard wall, she notices a motionless and tired man in

[19]See the introduction by William Archer who details the reception of the play in *Hannele: A Dream Poem by Gerhart Hauptmann,* William Archer, translator, London: Heinemann, 1894.

whose eyes are "the fires of grief, like candles for the dead." She intuitively senses a kindred soul in need of consolation, "Is it because your mother, too, has died?" Immersed in thought, the stranger startles the child with his unresponsiveness and by his failure to support her hope that she again will see her mother in heaven. Hauptmann's Hannele and Rilke's orphan are placed in a depressed environment; naturalistically rendered, the children have a plausibly naive imagination. But where Hauptmann's Hannele sees Christ in a fever dream as a figure of radiant hope, Rilke's orphan faces Christ's painfully noncommittal silence. When picturing the orphan's surroundings, Rilke's verse is stark and colloquial; when he pictures her flight into the imaginary the language glows with fairy tale touches. Sentiment and realism blend in the poem.

Quite another scene reaches the eyes and haunts the mind in the second—in the order of composition —of Rilke's poems, "Judenfriedhof," "The Jewish Cemetery." For Rilke a preoccupation with death and graveyards was literary as well as biographical.[20] The English graveyard poets bequeathed their symbols to the romanticists and countless imitators so that in time they became clichés. Spring over the graves, graveyard roses, and evocations of All-Souls-Day permeate Rilke's volume of lyrics called *Larenopfer*,[21] *Offering to the Lares* (1895), or offerings to the ancient household gods or spirits who demand remembrance and prayer. Yet in Rilke's hands clichés often, even in his early poetry, became transformed through his original talent. Among his favorite landmarks were the graveyards of the Carmelites, of the Benedictines,

the catacombs of Santa Maria della Vittoria, the graveyard near the military school, and those in Prague where the charm of the mysterious impelled him to invite Vally for occasional trysts. Refuge, tranquillity, links with the past, imaginative and suggestive associations by the mind were afforded by these visits. If a touch of morbidity may be ascribed to these visitational inclinations, they were only a trifle more serious than the nineteenth century New England custom of Sunday afternoons spent at cemeteries. For Rilke there was life among things dead as when he described a butterfly escaping the mouth of a stone angel and flowers breaking through the ground.

Artists, poets, photographers, and historians have been entranced—as was Rilke—by the tens of thousands of varied gravestones in Prague's Jewish cemetery which dates back to the early part of the fifteenth century. All historical styles from the Gothic on are represented here in jumbled array; inscriptions and pictographs reveal the names of the old inhabitants,

18

[20]Revealing is Rilke's own statement: "These November days are always Catholic days for me. The second day of November is All Soul's Day which until my sixteenth or seventeenth year, wherever I may have been living, I always spent in graveyards, by unknown graves, by relatives and ancestors, by graves which I could not explain and upon which I had to meditate in the growing winter nights. It was probably then that the thought first came to me that every hour we live is an hour of death for someone, and that there are probably even more hours of death than hours of the living. Death has a dial with infinitely many figures." (Letter to Paula Becker, November 5, 1900). In the *Visions of Christ* are several cemetery and graveside scenes and backdrops.

[21]SW I, pp. 8-69.

the sun plays shadow tricks, and the general melancholic atmosphere gives credence to the many legends that survived over the long years.[22] One of these is told in a balladlike form by Rilke in one of the *Larenopfer* poems, "Rabbi Löw." After 1572 Judah Löw became one of the most celebrated chief rabbis of Prague; held in esteem by King Rudolf of Bohemia, he also was an intimate of such notables as the scientists Tycho Brahe and Johann Kepler. The tradition of his wisdom and powers was still rife in the Prague of the 1890's. In Rilke's ballad, Rabbi Löw wrests from the dead the secret of why an epidemic of children's death has struck the community. The dishonoring of marriage by adults has brought the plague—literally and symbolically—upon the children; once the guilty are punished, the plague is lifted. In Rilke's work the ties—imaginary and real—between the dead and the living are strong.

For the "Judenfriedhof" poem in the Christ cycle, Rilke relied on the well-known legends of Rabbi Löw's supernatural powers, especially exhibited through the Prague Golem who was created from clay by the use of God's name; the Golem was an avenging figure who protected the persecuted of the ghetto.[23] It is at the wise rabbi's grave that Jesus, "the poor Jew, not the redeemer," confronts the graybeard God and his powerful follower. The rhetorical monologues are bitter, disillusioned, accusatory and picture Christ's frustrations at having brought God's word to man in vain, at not having been able to find manifestations of God, and at the inability—even at Gethsemane—to create God through love and anguish. From the rabbi he harshly demands a curse, an alchemical fire, a poison which will drive mankind to an orgy of love or hate, bringing about an apocalypse. Possibly Rilke refers to Luke's Christ who prophecies doom, "the Kingdom of God is at hand," or he intimates here the apocryphal belief that the Messiah will come when the world sinks into total corruption. Better this, seems to be the inference, than putting up with the present madness of the world. The declamatory eloquence of the lines reminds one of the visual rhetoric of Rubens' painting *Christ Wishing to Destroy the World.*

Quite forced is the analogy, "is there no poison sweet as mother's kiss," but for Rilke the image of a mother or pleasure-seeking wife is autobiographically obsessive. In an earlier retelling of a countryside legend, he wrote: "In a moment of desperation, Swanhilde infatuated with a young squire poisoned her husband—not as wives nowadays in similar cases poison life, but through wine."[24] These stinging casual-seeming references were part of Rilke's private grievances.

Anger and anguish swell toward climaxes in the lines:

19

[22]Superb photographs may be found in *The Old Prague Jewish Cemetery*, text by Jindrich Lion, photographs by Jan Lukas, Prague: Artia, 1960, as well as in the photo collection by Karl Plicka, mentioned in the acknowledgments.

[23]That the traditional lore was still generally rife in the Prague of the 1890's is noted by David Philipson, *Old European Jewries*, Philadelphia: Jewish Publication Society, 1894, pp. 113-14.

[24]SW V, pp. 296-97.

Und in der Menschen irres Wahngewimmel
Warf deinen Namen ich—das grosse "Er."

And when mankind in frenzied mobs would rave,
Your name—the great "He"—unto them I threw.

Rhetorical retardation through punctuation, inversions, accelerations and gruff, clashing syllables—"irres Wahngewimmel"—are marks of a technique through which the poet seeks mastery of his dramatic material. Stylistically, as in most of the other poems in the Christ cycle, "Judenfriedhof" shows Rilke's experimentation and virtuosity in media other than the earlier lyrics that showed traces of Schiller, Goethe, and Heine.

20 "Munich," wrote Rilke after leaving Prague, "has tempted so many creative minds because despite its sociability it remains a city of loneliness for the serious." For the first time in his young life he could choose between sociability and loneliness as he wished. He recorded the color and sportiveness of "the constant celebration of the folk and their participation in all festive joys. The golden autumn brings madcap days to the October meadows whose bright display booths bring joy particularly to the big children. . . ."[25] Like a magnet the traditional annual October festival and fair in Munich at Theresa Field attracted Rilke. And quite graphically in the poem "Jahrmarkt" he narrates, "It was at the October festival . . . ," brilliantly evoking the hurly-burly mood of the fair. In tempo, tune, and lifelikeness it reminds one of Goethe's scene "Vor dem Tor," "Before the City Gate," in *Faust*. Both Goethe and Rilke were able to turn the dross of the "Knittelvers" technique, a varia-

tion of the low-esteemed doggerel, into a delightful poetic form that capitalizes on rapidity of meter and ingenuity of end-line rhymes. Rilke's bantering and gay lines depend for their seeming rapidity of meter on the activeness of the verbs and on the soft stressing of such accented syllables as "an . . . ihre . . . sie . . . kehrt . . . bot . . . aus," creating the marvelously light and subtle effects he intended.

Rilke as narrator in "Jahrmarkt" is drawn into the past as he enters a booth bearing the placard "The story of Christ Jesus and His Passion." Inside, the wax exhibits consist of scenes from the birth at Bethlehem, Joseph's flight, in disputation at the Temple, the entrance into Jerusalem, the trial, and the crucifixion. An eerie silence reigns as the narrator moves from scene to scene. In the trial tableau Christ appears ennobled by deep woe, a pale and thorn-crowned majestic figure who pleads, "behold, this is man," only to have the mob demand that he be put to the cross. Suddenly the wax figure on the cross seems to show life and groans, in the words of the Psalms, Matthew, and Mark: "Why hast thou, oh my God, forsaken me?" Rilke's Christ blames his boastful disciples for his involuntary resurrection to serve their ends, his impalement on churches and exhibition at gaudy fairs, eternally dying from cross to cross, finding no resting place and suffering the paradox of being assailed by distasteful and impossible prayers despite his strengthlessness. Scarcely has a poet more bitterly attacked some of the work of Christ's followers and what Rilke thought to be their invented orthodoxy, fanatic-

[25]Translated from SW V, p. 330.

ism, and martyrdom symbolized by the blood of Christ.

Toward the end of 1896 and during his first few months in Munich, Rilke finished two more poems in the cycle—"Der Narr," contextually translated as "The Loon" (close to mad vagabond rather than "the fool or jester") and the poem "Die Nacht," "The Night."

In "Der Narr," a light tone perfectly captures groups of young children at carefree play after being let out of school captivity. A youthful Mars pulls the ribbon on the braid of one of the girls and runs from the barrage of female shouts. When a tall figure with a pale face appears, so unlike the iconographical one of Christ to which they are accustomed, they disperse with an alarmed cry, "the loon." Sound-words like "Wortgewirr" and "Stimmgeschnarr" reproduce the confusion. Breathlessly, Rilke's lines shorten as the stranger frantically seeks out Anna, the daughter of Mary Magdalene. He asks the child—who does not know her father but believes him to be in heaven—to repeat the word "Papa." She does and a cry of jubilation breaks from him but it quickly turns to sadness, "I cannot give you anything/. . . I am much poorer than you are, girl." Only momentarily had he yielded to the paternal instinct and human yearnings. The denouement of the poem brings one up short with its dramatic-recognition lines.

Theologians and writers have drawn from the composite and in detail differing biographies of Christ in the Gospels to portray either the divine or the human aspects of Christ. Rilke chose the trend which discards the supernatural and views Christ in human dimensions as did many other modern writers, most notably D. H. Lawrence and Nikos Kazantzakis. The theme of the resurrection and its aftermath furnished material for fictive speculation. Lawrence's version, although much later and more sensational, may be compared with Rilke's. In an essay, "The Risen Lord," Lawrence writes,

> Christ risen in the flesh! We must accept the image complete, if we accept it at all. . . . It is only the image of our own experience. Christ rises, when He rises from the dead, in the flesh, not merely as spirit. He rises with hands and feet, as Thomas knew for certain: and if with hands and feet, then with lips and stomach and genitals of a man. Christ risen in the whole of His flesh, not with some left out.

Christ if resurrected, according to Lawrence, would continue to fight social battles but also enjoy life to the fullest: "Life is lovely."[26] He characterized "The

21

[26]After coming across an essay on religion by D. H. Lawrence, Rilke wrote to his publisher Anton Kippenberg, December 5, 1924, telling him that he had read the essay many times over and that phrases in it reminded him of his own letter-essay "Remembrances of Verhaeren" and his "Workman's Letter" (written in February 1922 but only published posthumously in 1930). These writings are polemics directed against those who, in Rilke's view, misunderstand the meaning of God, Christ, life, death. God is a conviction within Rilke and not something learned. Metaphorically Rilke sees Christ as a tree in God on which we could ripen like fruit. The teachings of the Old Testament, the Koran, Christ are all pointers to God; Christ is a pointer, a gesture, and not a dwelling place. Had Lawrence known of Rilke's views, he would have agreed that "the church has embezzled this world for one in the beyond" and assented to the Rilke statement that "to a heart that has comprehended this earth, the view that one is sinful and needs ransom as a premise for God is more and more repugnant" (Letter to Ilse Jahr, February 22, 1923).

Escaped Cock" (also called "The Man Who Died") as "a story of the Resurrection, where Jesus gets up and feels very sick about everything, and can't stand the old crowd anymore—so cuts out . . . as he heals up, he begins to find what an astonishing place the phenomenal world is, far more marvellous than any salvation or heaven—and thanks his stars he needn't have 'a mission' any more." In the story the waxlike figure with the dead white face says, "I am not dead. They took me down too soon. So I have risen up. Yet if they discover me, they will do it all over again." It is almost as if the voice of Dostoevsky's jesuitical Grand Inquisitor were speaking to say that Christ in the modern world would be martyred all over again. Lawrence's Christ wants his own life and suffers nausea in thinking about man's inverted values in acclaiming the corpse rather than the body of Christ:

> It was fear, the ultimate fear of death, that made men mad. So always he [Christ] must move on. . . . There was nothing he could touch, for all, in a mad assertion of the ego, wanted to put a compulsion on him, and violate his intrinsic solitude. It was the mania of cities and societies and hosts, to lay a compulsion upon a man, upon all men. For men and women alike were mad with the egotistic fear of their own nothingness. And he thought of his own mission, how he tried to lay the compulsion of love on all men. And the old nausea came back on him.

The second part of the story becomes a fantasy as the Lady of Isis and Christ, symbolically the reincarnation of the god Osiris, celebrate bodily love; in the blaze of his manhood, he calls out, "I am risen."

If Lawrence's work was attacked as travesty in the 1930's, one can well imagine the reception which would have been accorded Rilke's "Die Nacht," "Night," had he decided to publish the poem. Rilke's re-creation has sharp and realistic edges, with few traces of lyricism, in secularizing Christ. The night mood is quickly rendered as, in the satirically named inn room "To the Angels," "Time drips gradually through the clock." Christ's temptations, "his cravings, that so long were held at bay, now burst their bond" and are consumed with a woman. Strong in his memory is the prosecution before the crucifixion and he recounts the event as if in a daze. The Gospels differ somewhat in the questions and answers given so that Rilke's version is an amalgam with an added psychological interpretation. At first, Christ's answer is evasive but then it rises to the affirmative under the goading of immense pride. To the woman, Christ repentantly confesses that he is no god; she readily agrees but assures him ribaldly that after a night with her he will be a king in the morning. Points of identification by Rilke with Christ are evident. We remember the military school episode where his pride rises to shrill heights as it did in *Ewald Tragy*. More subtle is Rilke's Don Juanism[27] which takes as one of its prototypes the love of Mary Magdalene for Christ[28]—

[27]Don Juanism in the life and work of Rilke has not escaped biographers and critics. This aspect is concisely reviewed by W. L. Graff, *Rainer Maria Rilke: Creative Anguish of a Modern Poet*, Princeton: Princeton University Press, 1956, pp. 173-79.

[28]Rilke's idea of Christ—with outstretched arms on the cross—being a marker or pointer (Wegweiser) to God and Mary Magdalene as a figure possessing almost unbearable love is strikingly rendered in his descriptive essay on Rodin's "Christus und Magdalena" (SW V, pp. 255-56).

22

significantly, she was the first person to whom he was to appear after the resurrection; Rilke was not above mildly boasting of his powers of attraction and being able to take or leave the respondent. The "Night" poem moves on two levels: crude, frenetic action and poetic symbolism. Christ's temptation is portrayed crassly, in contrast to the nostalgic wish to have been a father in "Der Narr." Here the conflict breaks out openly between affirmation and negation, a divine mission—spirit—and sexuality. Poetically and symbolically, the dawn's arrows strike through pale windows, to nail the planks with spears, the crown of thorns becomes a garland of roses, and water becomes wine, champagne. Emotions and actions are driven to the extremes reflected in the variations from banality of language to imaginative metaphor. The all-too-human portraits, bordering on the sensational, are at the service of Rilke's vision of Christ's ambivalence.

During Rilke's early months in Munich, he was fortunate in meeting the remarkable novelist Jakob Wasserman who, despite his exterior gruffness, took a liking to the young poet from the "provinces." René's contact with Wasserman was salutary and sobering, especially while writing the *Visions* which required a realistic tone. To Wasserman, life had been a severe task-master and his talks with Rilke were antidotes to the poet's habits of self-pity. Wasserman told him that a writer must forget about big, meaningless words and false phrases and become an unremitting worker; hatred or disapproval are signs that one is *not* being pitied; sympathy one must regard as a bore; and the writer's occupation is *Schauen*, observation of life. Still, part of René's mind was in Prague and the need for self-justification was strong. As a sign of achievement, René sent to his father a copy of his newly-published poetry collection *Traumgekrönt, Crowned with Dreams*—written earlier—with an inscription intending to give "new proof of the honesty of my artistic striving," signed in conciliatory fashion, "Your very much long-indebted René." Originally, he had planned to include a section of Christ poems in *Traumgekrönt*, but these were not ready in time nor were they of the same impressionistic style, mood, and meaning.

In Rilke's early upbringing was a heavy stress on the spiritual, yet once having cast off the sacred symbols—Christ, the protective childhood angel, the saints—toward which devotional feelings had been directed, his interest still was magnetized by unseen forces, the mysterious beyond the ken of human knowledge, the feeling of closeness to the dead as encouraged by graveyard visits, and intimations of extra-terrestrial spirits either as residues of intuition or as creatures of the imagination. The earthy and the unearthly coexisted in Rilke's mind. Without orthodox symbols the spiritual can become the basis for spiritualism, a direction toward which Rilke momentarily thought he might be turning. The philosophy of spiritualism appealed to René in its idealistic view of the material body as illusion and as a product or manifestation of spirit—the absolute reality. Spiritualism, at that time, seemed to hold possibilities for Rilke as a religion for those who find themselves outside of all religions and as a system which allows belief in communication

23

with the unseen world, immortality, and survival after death. With these ideas in mind, René wrote to Karl Baron Du Prel, a psychic investigator and philosopher who believed man to be dualistic in that he has another self which can shuttle to the beyond independent of his corporeal state. Rilke said:

> Apart from the charm of the mysterious, the domains of spiritualism have for me an important power of attraction because in the recognition of the many idle forces and in the subjugation of their power I see the liberation of our remote descendants and believe that in particular every artist must struggle through the misty fumes of crass materialism to those spiritual intimations that build for him the golden bridge into shoreless eternities . . . it will perhaps be vouchsafed me sometime to become with word and pen one of the adherents of the new faith that towers high above church-steeple crosses . . . it seems to me that in my "Visions of Christ," appearing this year, I shall come a big step nearer to your group. (February 16, 1897)

Several things stand out in the letter: Rilke's search for a "new faith"— which was to be subsumed eventually under the rubric of art; a will to dominate both the world of creativity and the personal world; and his intention to publish the Christ poems. A letter to Ludwig Ganghofer on April 16, 1897, confirmed the information that five Christ poems were destined for publication in Michael Conrad's periodical *Die Gesellschaft,* but that for the rest there was as yet no publisher. Nothing was to come of those intentions.

In the meantime his quest continued for "the new faith that towers high above church-steeple crosses," a quest, as he wrote in a poem for Du Prel, "to the pale stars/along the path which longing leads me."[29] One result, in April/May, was a brilliant technical performance in blending mood and idea in the poem "Venedig," "Venice." One of Christ's stops is the Doge's palace whose upper-story chambers were notorious as a state prison dating from the time of the Venetian Republic. From one of its windows, Silvio Pellico, author of the play *Francesca da Rimini* which retold the legend of the illicit and ill-fated love of Paolo and Francesca, had peered into the courtyard of the palace and at St. Mark's gigantic campanile. The story of Pellico's incarceration in the 1820's for being a member of the Carbonari who sought to free Italy from Austrian despotism is told in his memoirs *I Mie Prigioni (My Prisons).* His survival of a ten-year ordeal is attributable to his unexpected conversion to religion and adoption as his ideal the patiently suffering Christ figure on Mount Golgotha, "the friend of the unhappy and the friend of man." Christ acknowledges symbolically the affinity with Pellico whose passions were tamed and worn out by chains and woe. But at the heart of Rilke's "Venice" poem is a long dialogue between Christ and an imagined Venetian elder whose prayer and "kneeling seemed to grow out far/past Christ." The elder tells Christ that his teachings are rich feasts that draw receptive guests who are made to forget temporal misery and to pray blindly like children. A majestic and discursive mood pervades the dialogue as two friendly adversaries calmly and honestly exchange views. The magistrate speaks wearily but firmly,

> Doch ich bin alt. Ich seh die Zeiten rollen
> bis in den Tag, da keine Völker mehr

[29]SW III, 556 f.

wie Kinder sein und Kinder spielen wollen;
denn mögen alle deine Glocken grollen,
dann bleibt auch dein Palast für ewig leer.

But I am old. I see the seasons turning
until the day when nations will no more
for childhood's way and childhood play be yearning;
then, even though your bells keep up their churning,
the dust will gather on your palace-floor.

Rilke's Utopia is somewhat like that of the French romanticists who saw the ideal state of the future as being one of harmony and without dogma and rite. Neither "Venice" nor the other poems in the Christ cycle were spiritualistic, despite what was implied in the letter to Du Prel. Rilke's relation to spiritualism and seances was to be complex. The over-all impression one receives is that his attitude was both circumspect and ironic, that he was more vividly touched by the superstitions regarding spirits than the tenets of spiritualism, but that certain spiritualistic ideas mingled with antique mythology and intuitive speculation to give us a grand vision of the beyond in his culminating *Duino Elegies*.

Rilke took Wasserman's suggestion that he read the works of the Danish novelist Jens Peter Jacobsen, and in short order Jacobsen became René's "guide for my heaven on earth," a corroborator of ideas which René had already formed tentatively. Through the semi-autobiographical novel *Niels Lyne* and the historical novel *Fru Marie Grubbe*, Jacobsen preached the right of the individual to exist in his own way and to revolt against religion by substituting an unsentimental and inexorably Darwinian view of nature shorn of divine agents that forgive repentant sinners. Jacob-

sen stressed the tranquil, self-directed life, the dominance of childhood memories, and exhibited a fascination for the mystery of maidenhood. When René's absorption with these themes threatened to lead to rudderless introspection, gloom, and imbalance, Wasserman helped bring René to keel by directing him towards a woman of brilliant mind, a former confidante of Nietzsche and who was to be one of the earliest adherents of psychoanalysis, namely Lou Andreas-Salomé; she was married in name only, was fifteen years older than René, and was seasoned in the ways of the world. Noting certain similarities between Rilke's *Visions* and an essay by Lou called "Jesus der Jude," "Jesus the Jew," in the *Neue Deutsche Rundschau* (April 1896), Michael Conrad, the editor who had read parts of the *Visions* and expected to publish them, called Rilke's attention to the essay which heightened René's eagerness to meet Lou. Many of her conclusions he could readily agree with. Among the ideas she broached was that only the lone man, like Christ, "the great solitary, reaches the heights of religion, its true bliss and fullest tragedy; what he experiences there escapes the crowd below; his tragic end and his tragic perception remain as mysterious and as individualistic as his inspiration and oneness with God—they belong outside of history." In the religious genius and consuming faith of Jesus is solved the contradiction of man kneeling before a man-created God. Jesus became the Christ when godlike he shaped a new religion. What was the private agony of Christ on the cross, despairing of the existence of God, became transformed by his followers

25

into a public symbol of religious martyrdom. Primitive Christian theology arose from the fear of death and the unknown and from a mighty yearning for belief in the hereafter; its creation of a heavenly Jesus has no relation to the solitary genius who receives and tells of a God-revelation through the deepest inner spirituality. Lou saw Jesus not as a conqueror but as the sharpest expression of Judaism's emotional anthropomorphism. Further she suggested that religious experience achieves validity only in living, feeling, and empathically suffering God solely through the emotions.

René told Lou jubilantly in his first letter to her —May 13, 1897—that she had masterfully expressed the very ideas of his "dream epics" (Traumepen) in the *Christus-Visionen*: "Your essay related to my poems like dream to reality, like a wish to its fulfillment." It did not take long before René enthusiastically read the *Visions* to Lou. Eventually she became his substitute mother, mistress, and intellectual companion in a relationship which proved René's persuasiveness. Reciprocally, at her prompting, he dropped the name René in his signed works in favor of Rainer; the name René, close to the feminine Renée, had been given to him by his mother because of her frustrated wish to have another girl for the one who had died and her inclination for French culture. In the role of Rainer, he felt a new freedom and maturity; in his further occupation with the figure of Christ, he was impressed with the power of inner confidence in pursuit of an outer mission whether in the direction of religion or, as in his own case, poetry.

In the summer of 1897, Rainer wrote "Die Kinder," "The Children," a poem in which adoring youngsters, and adults in the periphery, crowd around the radiant iconographical figure of Christ, seeking his blessings. His sermon, however, contains some sobering paradigms:

Ihr wollt ins Leben, und das bin ich nicht,
ihr müsst ins Dunkel, und ich bin das Licht.
ihr hofft die Freude, ich bin der Verzicht,
ihr sehnt das Glück und—ich bin das Gericht.

I am not life, and life is what you are after;
the darkness is your portion—I illume;
'Renounce!' I cry—but you are lured by laughter;
you crave good fortune,—and my voice is doom.

Rilke is touched by the simple faith of sheltered children but is aware that it will have to give way, as it did for him, when confronting life. Childhood illusions obviously serve up to a point in the natural development of the individual; beyond that point, Rilke seems to imply, each person must seek for himself the meaning of life and death. The way of Christ may not be the way for all men in that Christ's lonely mission was a despairing one even for himself. Rilke's Christ is inspired by Matthew's portrayal which glows with affection for children: "Suffer little children, and forbid them not, to come unto me; for such is the kingdom of heaven." Those who seek Christ, says Rilke, can find him metaphorically in scenes of childhood—a mother's smile, a moment of expectancy. In that sense can the following statement of Rilke's Christ be understood: "I am Memory and Childhood."

The theme of Christ and the children lends itself to pathos and tenderness rendered by the infinitely soft alliterations and gliding rhymes in the dreamlike lines.

Some of Rilke's poetic pictorializations of Christ scenes were inspired by and adapted from the paintings of the once well-known artist Fritz von Uhde (1848-1911). Today, Uhde's prolific and largely representational output seems passé.[30] In one of Uhde's devotional portraits, Christ graphically illuminates the darkness and represents light as does the figure in Rilke's "The Children." In Munich Rilke sporadically attended lectures on art history at the university. Yet his taste in art developed strongly only after he met Rodin, felt the impact of Cézanne and Picasso, and turned his attention from subject to form. Rilke was fascinated by the Christ themes in Uhde's work. Uhde went the gamut from realism, imitational baroque devotionalism, to impressionism—sometimes expressing his own vision of life and sometimes acceding to public tastes. Some of Uhde's Christ paintings departed from the tradition of pictorial splendor by bringing Christ close to contemporary surroundings, especially to the peasant folk, and by giving him simple dress descriptive of no single period. Undoubtedly, Uhde found precedent in the humanization of Biblical figures by Rubens and the stress on moral expression rather than physical beauty by Rembrandt. Greater than his finished and smoothed-out paintings, his sketches show Uhde to have been a painter who could have transcended his time had he the will and self-confidence that makes of art an absolute mission. Rilke thought that the best of

Uhde's work was that in which children played a role and in which Uhde indirectly captured the Christ figure of love and faith and refuge as reflected in their eyes.

Rilke's deeply subjective description of Uhde's Christ picture called *Let the Children Come unto Me* holds particular interest because it shows the mood and portraiture which Rilke attempted in his poem "The Children:"

> In "Let the Children come unto Me," it was the concern of the painter to give the wishes and dreams of these children a common focal point, to create a pair of rich and kind hands stretched out toward the hesitant questions and search of these helpless hands, lips which can give consolation and answer to the thousand boundless and bold questions of children, and to create an eye which is radiant enough to become a homeland to those who come out of the dark. He wanted to make the children a gift of a father without the worries, agedness, or anger of a father; in short, to fulfill the deepest and most mysterious longings of their tiny, awakening souls.[31]

Rilke prefers the Uhde paintings in which the onlookers reveal by *their* emotions the presence of Christ, to those in which Christ and the onlookers are grouped conventionally. Unfortunately Uhde was pliable when attacked by philistine demands for conventional renderings so that when his painting of the *Holy Night* (1888) was castigated for allegedly showing in his Madonna "the features of a prostitute

27

[30]A comprehensive descriptive and pictorial purview of Uhde's work may be found in *Uhde: Des Meisters Gemälde in 285 Abbildungen*, edited by Hans Rosenhagen, Stuttgart und Leipzig: Deutsche Verlags-Anstalt, 1908.

[31]Translated from "Uhde's Christus," SW V, pp. 351-57.

who has brought her child into the world in a dive," he promptly beautified Mary's face, tidied up her surroundings, and added symbolical iconographic devices. Similar concessions were made when the influential Munich gallery, the Pinakothek, offered to purchase Uhde's painting "The Ascension of Christ" (1897) provided that he accent the Christ figure and its ascent. Rilke published a biting article about the stipulation, noting that Uhde's earlier redeeemer was "in no way acquainted with all the finesses of flight techniques."

Rilke also mentioned in the article that he had visited Uhde's studio in November 1896 and that he had seen the preliminary painting—a superbly dynamic rendering on gray canvas with turbulent charcoal strokes and vast space over the heads of the crowd. The phenomenon of belief and its power attracted Rilke; apparently Uhde's preliminary sketch spoke to him in those terms:

> Imagine if you will a group of people—not of peasants and not of the educated but simply of people: the elderly, men, maiden, and women. And, imagine this group to be forcibly drawn together, united and commonly enthralled by *one* sensation. In fine shading on all the faces is the effect of something great and incredible: wonderment in the women, in the maiden; glorification in the children, trust . . . And then in their hands — in that of the elderly, doubt; fear in those of men and women, longing in the hands of maiden; and the hands of children half-unconsciously imitate the gesture of the wondrous one . . .

Rilke scorned the officially sanctioned ascension which Uhde agreed to paint by touching up and changing his original work: "it proves that basically he no longer sees Christ very clearly." In the new version, the painter dissociates himself from the crowd and gives it the conventional "Jesus" rather than Christ, "the redeemer who humanly and modestly was on solid ground" in earlier Uhde paintings.

It was at about this time that Rilke wrote his poem "Der Maler," "The Painter," in which Christ and a painter, modelled only vaguely on Uhde, engage in a sharp exchange; like all sound writers, Rilke gives definition to both of the characters in conflict. The continuity between the poems "The Children" and "The Painter" is made clear in Christ's sensitivity for children, which in contrast this painter seems to lack. The painter, after a struggle with shame and guilt inspired by Christ's arguments, throws off the "slave" bonds of timidity and claims that he has always seen Christ in beggar's garbs.[32] At this, Christ draws himself up in full dignity, as in the other Rilke poems, and goaded by fierce pride proclaims the sanctity of his solitary being, his chosen royal lineage: only after he died did he become a slave. The paradox is elucidated when Rilke's Christ notes that divinity no longer is divinity when it becomes subject to the

[32]The same struggle and disillusionment is evident in Rilke's poem "Du . . . ," written in Munich, November 12, 1896 and printed a year later. Translated by Aaron Kramer it reads:

> Henceforth I cannot but remember.
> As lately you appeared in slumber,
> with wounded wrists you came toward me
> down from a crimson Calvary.
>
> "Forgive my taunts!" in fear I cried—
> you seized the scar that burned your side:
> "I bring a rose to you," he said,
> And handed me a drop of red. . . (SW III, p. 447)

demands of mass man. Rilke's lines, "Then I became —a god. And only those/among the gods are great, whom no one knows," echo Swinburne's poetic aphorism, "God whom we see not, is; and God who is not, we see."[33] Rilke's Christ again declares himself king of children—the manifestation in memory and childhood. Some of Rilke's own conflicts and problems of articulating and pictorializing aspects of Christ are mirrored in the painter.

After the composition of "The Children" and "The Painter," Rilke wrote to the publisher Adolf Bonz on December 25, 1897: ". . . poems, which accompany every phase of my spiritual longing, are experiences through which I ripen . . . poems are gifts to everyone, presents, bounties . . . I cannot keep my springtime silent in order to give it out some day in summer, old and faded. . . ." Rilke's *Visions* arose out of inner need and reflected his intellectual growth, but he chose not to present the Christ poems as gifts to a public who would have resented the exotic bouquet. Instead he gave them, at the time, fairly conventional bounties with sparse ideas—shimmering with melodious songlike poems—in his volumes *Advent, Traumgekrönt* (*Crowned with Dreams*), and *Mir zur Feier* (*In My Honor*). Some of the easily digestible volumes of verse published during his Munich and Berlin days received—on the whole— excellent reviews as poetry displaying high lyrical quality and he basked in the tributes.[34] Rilke was willing enough to criticize Herr Fritz von Uhde and his religious platitudes, yet himself was unwilling to defy mass taste and convention. Rilke allowed a comfort-

able but incomplete image of himself to be presented to the public. To support this view, one need only compare the two different poems on "Venice" in *Advent*[35] and in the *Visions*, which have similar imagery, and to compare the diametrically opposed views of Christ in the *Visions* with the short cycle "Funde," "Inventions," in *Advent*. With pictorial delicacy the Christ of *Advent* becomes a figure of repose, a dreamer on the cross toward whom reach slim, white, and soothing hands of jasmine; his miracles still reign.[36] No trace is here of Rilke's dynamically interpreted Christ figure in the *Visions*. The dichotomy between the private view and that made public in Rilke's works is rarely more evident.

Rilke's life in Munich—when he chose—was as full as that in Prague, considering his writing, lecturing, and meeting colorful personalities. But again there seemed to be something too indiscriminate about all this activity until the spring of 1898 when he went briefly to Italy; there he literally collected his thoughts in what has been called the *Tuscan Diaries*. Renaissance masters inspired Rilke by the greatness of their art, their creativeness and productivity. There he reinforced his ideas of the artist's role almost in religious terminology as the poet usurps the function and mission of the Creator. The esthetically oriented

29

[33]SW VI, pp. 1323-24, contains a list, including Swinburne, indicative of the young Rilke's reading interests.

[34]Demetz, p. 6, *passim*. Demetz discusses the rave reviews and more moderate ones of Rilke's lyrical poetry.

[35]SW I, p. 116.

[36]SW I, p. 122.

Fritz von Uhde's three-panel painting
Die Heilige Nacht, Holy Night.
The first version, 1888.

Fritz von Uhde's three-panel painting
Die Heilige Nacht, Holy Night.
The second version, 1889.

art of Botticelli,[37] who merged pagan and Christian symbols in a spirit of secular religiosity, made a powerful impact upon Rilke. Never a strong systematic or philosophical thinker, Rilke lets his feelings shape the thought of his poetry so that sometimes it wanders between pantheism and metaphysics without drawing upon niceties of distinction. Yet what emerged from his Italian sojourn was a finer sensibility and an inclination toward much greater poetic subtleties as is evident in the last three poems of the *Visions*, written in July 1898.

The three poems—among those which, Rilke told the publisher Bonz, would close the cycle[38]—exhibit no fierceness and no stridency; instead, a passive and disillusioned tone courses through them. In "The Church of Nago," situated in a small, poverty-stricken village near Lake Garda—between Venice and Lombardy whose landscape and vineyards are celebrated for their beauty—Christ hopes to find in his journey "from distant years" the old, simple faith which he had preached. His homecoming is not triumphal, but the memory that "the poor had once carried their hymns" here gives new strength to his weary limbs. Why the desuetude of religion and its neglect? Is it because the villagers pray elsewhere; are they resigned to death which comes whether or not it is placated with an expensive and unaffordable mass?[39] The immense suggestiveness which Rilke was able to pack into simple lines is astonishing:

Und die Ewigkeit, die er ausgespannt,
reicht nicht einmal von Wand zu Wand,
wird eine ängstliche Ewigkeit:
denn das Leben ist breit.

Und der Bleiche bleibt einsam an sein Rand,
bleibt knien.

And eternity, which he tried to spread
from wall to wall, is not wide enough,
becomes an eternity overawed:
because life is broad.
And the pale one stays alone at the rim,
kneeling.

Symbolically a nativity scene transfigures the last lines of the poem from reality to illusion with the implication that Christ's original work and teaching must either be regarded as lost in the modern world or that they need to be introduced all over again.

"Der Blinde Knabe," "The Blind Lad" is an imaginative ballad in which the youngster—Christ's name is not mentioned in the poem—wanders from door to door, graced with his mother's beauty. The lad cannot see, but Mary does, that his songs bring sorrow. His songs are so deeply moving that people give him alms and sympathy. But when he gently rejects these and offers his songs as gifts, he is turned away by the women who fear that their own children may be affected by the sightless one. The boy's pride

[37]In a letter to Frieda von Bülow, August 13, 1897, Rilke comments on the Botticelli madonnas, "heralds of his own sadness and weariness," melancholy figures "upon whose laps plays that little boy who wants to become the Redeemer."

[38]SW III, p. 790, note.

[39]In April, 1898, and in March, 1899, Rilke visited the Lake Garda region which is the setting for "The Church of Nago" poem. A comparison of the poem and a long diary entry (*Briefe und Tagebücher*, 1899-1902; 1931 edition, pp. 207-211) shows Rilke's imaginative and selective reconstitution in poetry of an actual experience.

and knowingness is great: his songs, though penetratingly sweet, are sparks that will cause a conflagration. Despite its soft-seeming texture, this poem contains nettles, especially the idea that the Christlad's penetrating and sweet message becomes unbearable for many people because of its pathos and his willingness to give more than people would accept.

A number of poems written about 1897 contain the figures of nuns through which Rilke symbolically showed the incarceration of earthly emotions disguised as spiritual—both having the same roots—and frustrated longings. One of the poems addressed to Lou is an elaborate conceit built on the notion of liberating her from nunlike bondage with his arrival. Rilke's poem "The Nun," in the *Visions*, pictures the entanglements of sacred and secular love as evident in the dialogue and instinctive action of an older nun who has already given herself to the bridegroom Christ and a novitiate who wishes the same ecstatic experience.[40] In a gesture of embarrassed sensuality and stark pity, possibly seeking human love, the nun extends pleading and empty hands. Christ is only invisibly present in the poem and it may have seemed appropriate to Rilke to let the cycle rest on that note. The dramatic, muted gesture of the nun seems to cap the recurrent idea of the *Visions*: strength for existence without illusions cannot come from without; it must gather power from within.

*   *   *

The subject of publishing the *Visions* was opened and closed again several times. Replying to a request for periodical publication of the poems, Rilke wrote to his friend Wilhelm von Scholz on February 9, 1899: "I have many reasons for concealing the Christ portraits—for a long, long time. They are gestations which accompany me throughout life. For these reasons, forgive my not yielding to your request." Concealment and gestation are the key words in the reply, suggesting that the issues raised needed further exploration. Considerably later, Anton Kippenberg—who published a Rilke collection called *Die frühen Gedichte* (*Early Poems*)—asked the poet on January 8, 1912, to send him poems, previously published or not, for inclusion in a new volume of *Erste Gedichte* (*First Poems*). On impulse, Rilke mentioned the existence of the "Christusvisionen:"

> My wife, who at the moment is in Oberneuland, will search through a certain trunk and send me everything that might possibly meet your request. I believe, however, that aside from the *Visions of Christ*, nothing usable will come of the search. And these great poems [die grossen Gedichte] which I have not seen again for a long time, I must have about me for a while, and

[40]Of the several nun poems which appeared intermittently in Rilke's works, the one which comes closest in poignancy to "The Nun" in the *Visions*, is "Nonnen-Klage," "The Nun's Lament," written eleven years later. The question of Rilke's preoccupation with this theme relates, in the main, to the larger problem of emotional reciprocity between humans and between the human and the divine. Autobiographical roots are evident in Rilke's letter to Lou Andreas-Salomé, dated February 7, 1912. In the letter he interprets the relationship between Saint Angela of Foligno and Christ as one in which "Christ proved daily that he was always more ready to give than to receive," a parallel which Rilke drew with his own relationships and his own state of "not being able to receive." Of interest also in "The Nun" poem of the *Visions* are several mystical lines which are amplified later in Rilke's *Book of Hours*.

33

on my conscience, before they (almost fifteen years after their creation) are to appear among people . . . [textual omission marks].[41]

It seems evident that Rilke had no doubts about the publishability or merits of these great (or big) poems but almost immediately regretted having mentioned their existence because it brought up the old conflict about making his most private views public. Since the *Visions* were the poems which established the bridge between himself and Lou Andreas-Salomé, Rilke wrote to her that he would not think of publishing them without finding out what she thought of the venture. About a year-and-a-half later she answered by giving indication of the importance of the poems but without committing herself on the publication question:

> Yes, I have reread the *Visions of Christ* . . . and several completely marvelous connections have become evident to me for the first time. The details are too difficult to relate! In tone they are far removed from [the first two of] the *Duino Elegies* . . . yet how remarkable it is that everything you have written moves organically between the *Visions of Christ* of the past and the visions of the angels of the future [the rest of the elegies].[42]

On one other occasion we know of, Lou remembered the *Visions*. During the Christmas of 1909, Rilke had sent Lou a reproduction of the painting *Christ on the Cross* by the French impressionist Eugène Carrière (1849-1906), displayed in the Musèe du Luxembourg. (Seven years before, Rilke had been drawn to Carrière—and visited him as he had Uhde—because of the spiritual quality and painterly interpretation of Christ and had intended to write a book about him.) Lou put up the reproduction in her "blue room

34

with the bear rugs," and wrote Rilke of her enthusiasm:

> Do you still remember how the Christ legends were the first poetry which you read to me in aristocratic houses? Yes, this is the Jesus [Carrière's] whom I love, or even more this woman Mary who releases him on his cross and delivers him. She stifles her cry in these hands, herself remaining sound, true to nature, and ever ready to bear mortality for the sake of his great deed, his immortal act.

Lou's comment is valuable for it reflects her and Rilke's empathy for the human drama which Christ's life represents. After 1913, the *Visions* are not mentioned in their published correspondence and the cycle remained shrouded for another twenty-five years.

Fragmented excerpts and brief commentary on the Christ poems appeared in doctoral dissertations by Ruth Mövius (*R.M. Rilkes Stundenbuch*, Leipzig, 1937), and by Marianne Sievers (*Die biblischen Motive in der Dichtung R.M. Rilkes*, Berlin, 1938). Finally in 1959, the eleven poems were published in the authoritative *Rainer Maria Rilke: Sämtliche Werke*, volume III, more than sixty years after their original composition. So meager are the facts that we can only speculate as to the long series of delays that have marked the publication history of the poems.

[41]Letter to Anton Kippenberg, January, 1912.

[42]References to the Christ poems appear in *Rainer Maria Rilke—Lou Andreas-Salomé Briefwechsel*, edited by Ernst Pfeiffer, Zürich: Niehans, 1952, pp. 9 f., 241, 257, f., 300 f., 511 f. (H. F. Peters, *My Sister, My Spouse*, New York: Norton, 1962, pp. 213-15, conjectures that Rilke's "great" *Visions* were not released by the poet for publication because of the intimate links they formed to the period with Lou.)

At first Rilke probably felt that the poems were too blunt and personal an expression of his strong feelings, that his re-evaluation of the Christ figure not only might be misunderstood but too clearly understood, jeopardizing his public stock, and that the poems would antagonize his Catholic relatives and his father, the sources of his support. Throughout, Rilke asked himself not whether the poems of the *Visions* cycle were ripe but whether or not the *time* was ripe for their publication. Between 1913 and 1923, he showed little interest in publishing anything. When his crowning works—the *Duino Elegies* and *Sonnets to Orpheus*—finally appeared, he retained little interest in his early work and rightly felt that it paled by comparison with the elegies and sonnets. After his death in 1926, Rilke's poems and correspondence were released piecemeal and, from a scholarly standpoint, chaotically. When in conjunction with the Rilke Archives, Insel-Verlag finally began to publish its definitive edition of Rilke's work in 1955, much of the previously unpublished material came to light. Between the bold publication-announcement by Rilke in the Prague periodical *Moderne Dichtung* in 1897, "in Erscheinung begriffen, 'Christus-Visionen,' " and their appearance in the third volume of the *Sämtliche Werke* in 1959 lie the indecisions and decisions—at first of Rilke and then the archives—affecting the publication timing of the *Visions*.

* * *

Because of the late publication of the *Visions*, few critics have as yet tried to place them in the development of Rilke and to assess their intrinsic value. During Rilke's lifetime critics called him a lyricist, a god-seeker, a pantheist, and the like. R. H. Heygrodt found a religious orientation in Rilke's lyricism and noted that the existence of the *Visions* gave evidence of "how early Rilke's basic religious sensitivity was active."[43] Rilke shuddered at the idea of being made a captive between the covers of critical studies and strongly tried to discourage critics and biographers, as his relations with Ellen Key show most clearly.[44] Critical works after Rilke's death in 1926 were sparse and suffered from insufficiency of biographical data and correspondences; material released by official sources often was incomplete or maimed. As a result, Rilke's autobiographical idealization of a noble lineage dating to 1367 was accepted almost uncritically while unpublished works made for gaps that disallowed a true picture of his ideological range. Interest in Rilke

35

[43]Robert Heinz Heygrodt, *Die Lyrik Rainer Maria Rilkes*, Frieburg: Bielsfelds, 1921, p. 23. While Rilke claimed that he never read critical evaluations of his work, he did read Heygrodt's study. In a letter to the author, on December 28, 1921, Rilke protested intrusions into his early life and works without his own official guidance. The letter is important in demonstrating what Rilke wished to have critics and biographers believe. He preferred to have much of his childhood and early youth rendered in martyr colors although much of his own writing and the accounts by others dispute the poet's exaggerations.

[44]Ellen Key, "Rainer Maria Rilke: Ein Gottsucher," *Seelen und Werke*, translated into German by Marie Franzos, Berlin: S. Fischer, 1911. Miss Key stressed the "God-seeker" and Rilke's mystic-religious sense of life, although the poet begged her to refrain from categorizing an attitude that was already in the past.

Eugène Carrière's painting
Christ on the Cross.

became significant in England during the late thirties; in 1941 the first sound biographical study of Rilke appeared in the form of E. M. Butler's *Rainer Maria Rilke*. With insight and some shrewd guesswork, Professor Butler almost was able to bridge huge gaps, as in the case of the *Visions*. She wrote, "the *Christ Visions* of 1897 deal with various aspects of the tragedy of a man who was believed to be a God." Actually, her incomplete summary was based on the fragments quoted and the commentary appearing in the works by Mövius and Sievers. Their excerpts were to form the only source for partial knowledge of the text until 1959. Yet, the Mövius study fell under the pall of editorial emasculations and selected overemphasis, while of the Sievers study Erich Simenauer has said that it represented "a book disfigured by propagandistic censorship."[45] Those responsible at the time were severely condemned by Butler for playing politics during the Nazi *régime*.[46] Sievers and Mövius hammered at the theme that Rilke's work is not Christian as proven and reinforced by the *Visions* excerpts; moreover, Sievers indulged in unscholarly acrobatics to insist that Rilke was not only anti-Catholic but also anti-Semitic, implying his worth—as a poet and thinker—to the anti-Christian theism of the New Order. Such intellectual dishonesty hardly merits mention except as a vindication of the need by scholars for wide access to Rilke archive-material. If, as a result, so-called blemishes appear, they will not disfigure the poet nor mar his poetry.

Butler raised a question about Rilke, which has agitated other commentators as well: "Has the work of the greatest German poet since Hölderlin real religious validity; or is it merely the mysterious expression of a one-man dream?" She answered this tentatively: "The real bent of his genius, though he forced it into religious channels, was esthetic. So much so indeed that he magnified art into a religion at the dictates of that passionate self-assertion he was at such pains to disguise." The *Visions*, aside from containing some of Rilke's best poetry up until the writing of his *Book of Hours*, are valuable precisely because they contain no disguises or ambiguities as do the later poems. In several respects then, the *Visions* afford a base for the problematic relationships of esthetics, belief, religion, and validity in Rilke's poetry.

Among the most knowledgeable Rilke critics, Hans Egan Holthusen and Eudo C. Mason, display a profound hostility to the ideas which inform Rilke's poetry; at the same time, they admire the art evident in many of the poetic works. On the surface this attitude may seem contradictory, but it is not; it only proves the power of Rilke's poetry. However, it is arguable whether in fact one can dissociate the ideas from the art. Holthusen categorically states that "Rilke's 'ideas' are wrong and his idea of a world of pure inwardness is a heresy" as is the dissolving of God into intense feeling and that Rilke makes "all earthly and metaphysical realities" unreal. Further, he claims that Rilke, like Nietzsche and Baudelaire,

37

[45]Erich Simenauer, *Rainer Maria Rilke: Legende und Mythos*, Bern: Haupt, 1953, p. 48.
[46]E. M. Butler, *Rainer Maria Rilke*, Cambridge [Eng.]: Cambridge University Press, 1941, pp. 7-8.

belongs to a psychic type that is fundamentally Christian but that his consciousness, influenced by a long secular tradition, is anti-Christian.[47] Holthusen calls Rilke's love for figures of Christian legend not estheticism, as others have, but a calculated pose to destroy their meaning more effectively. Mason concludes from the *Visions of Christ* poems that "it emerges clearly that Rilke, like Nietzsche, and D. H. Lawrence, felt himself called upon to be a great Antichrist." This is somewhat stronger than a much earlier statement by Mason that "Rilke, exactly like other neo-heathen geniuses, inwardly possessed a secret Christian whom he constantly had to battle."[48] The salvationists' view of the pagan poet as an *anima naturaliter christians*, an instinctive Christian soul, had been a medieval and Renaissance device to make Homer, Plato, Ovid, and Vergil palatable and serviceable to the church, and it is a little startling to find it revived in the twentieth century and applied to Rilke. Casting still another interpretation upon Rilkean belief, the Catholic theologian Romano Guardini suggests that Rilke, like Hölderlin and Nietzsche, did not cull thoughts from his own center, but developed them in relation and in epiphenomenal opposition to Christian teachings in an "attempt to draw Christian existential elements into the purely secular."[49] Mason notes that almost all of Rilke's clear attacks on Christianity remained unpublished because of Rilke's growing preferences, after writing the *Visions*, for "subtle, quasi-mystical ambivalences" which prevented people from realizing his actual affinity with "the postulates of many of the advanced minds of his generation."

In some ways these were welcome voices in protest against a chorus composed of adulators who wished to make of Rilke a saint and a revealer of a new universal religion, who was sent into this world with a mission and sang of his nearness to God.[50] The late J. B. Leishman, who for better or for worse held a long-time monopoly on the translation of Rilke's poetry, was aware of the extreme and conflicting interpretations of Rilke's "religious" orientation and when asked about the translation of the *Christ Visions* into English strongly advised against it mainly on the grounds that the poems would provide ammunition for Rilke's so-called detractors.[51] Such timidity, aside from being tiresome, is obstructive and unproductive. One can only shove Rilke's ideas under the rug at the expense of misreading his poetry. Moreover, one may be justifiably impatient with the question of "real religious validity" since this is only answerable from a subjective point of

38

[47]Hans Egan Holthusen, *Rainer Maria Rilke: A Study of his Later Poetry*, translated by J. B. Stern, New Haven: Yale University Press, 1952, pp. 42-43.

[48]Eudo C. Mason, *Rilke*, London: Oliver and Boyd, 1963, p. 16; *Lebenshaltung und Symbolik bei Reiner Maria Rilke*, Weimar: H. Böhlaus, 1939, p. 65.

[49]Romano Guardini, *Zur RMRs Deutung des Daseins*, second edition, Bern, 1946, p. 59.

[50]Butler, p. 5. Katharina Kippenberg's memoir (RMR, Leipzig, 1948) is typical of the excessive adulation showered on Rilke. To her, Rilke reading from his *Duino Elegies* "looked as if he had descended from Mount Sinai," p. 329).

[51]Unpublished correspondence.

view and results in philosophical or religious sectarian vainglory. No one as yet has established a clear-cut monopoly of valid religious thought. For personal and intellectual reasons, the young Rilke experienced the disintegration of myths and symbols of his childhood and eclectically tried to salvage some and fuse them into a new vision. Such fusion and change accompanied his poetic output throughout life. Whether Rilke's thought was more pronounced in the direction of the esthetics of religion or the religion of esthetics is less important than the realization that his visions have a highly psychological and moralistic orientation. This should become evident when we place the *Visions* into the conceptual framework which the young Rilke was building.

Linked by some to the *Visions*, Rilke's short story "Der Apostel," "The Apostle," written in 1896, has caused no end of difficulty for Rilke biographers. Nora Wydenbruck described it as a "puerile gospel of Hate" composed under the influence of bad company (a ludicrous charge); Butler interpreted it as a "savage Nietzschean attack on Christ;" the critic W. L. Graff saw it as a reminder "that there was something hard and ruthless in Rilke's make-up,"[52] while others failed to see in it any relevance to the body of Rilke's work. Simenauer predicted that once Rilke's *Visions* were released the link to the "Apostel" would become apparent. The link now has become apparent, but not in the way suggested by most commentators. There is no doubt but that the young Rilke came under the influence of Nietzsche's philosophy of culture. One of Nietzsche's favorite precepts was that man must ceaselessly lose himself and find himself to avoid the staleness of a rigid point of view: "Become the person you really are." To Siegfried Trebitsch, a friend during the Prague castle days, Rilke had declared that it is one's sacred duty to fulfill God's eleventh commandment: Become what you are.[53] Transforming Nietzsche's commandment into God's meant only acceptance of part of Nietzsche's views: the need to transcend nationality, affirmation of life rather than the renunciation preached by some of Christ's followers who held out the reward of a life beyond the tomb and a "slave mentality" on earth; Nietzsche's "overman," the thoroughly independent and creative philosopher-ruler, was to become the symbol of the artist for the young Rilke. But whereas Nietzsche sought his fulfillment in ecstasy and in the solitary demonic isolation of his vision, which resulted in mental disintegration—he died under the illusion that he was the hammerer, Dionysus, the Crucified—Rilke was able to deal with the world on its own opportunistic terms. He made concessions where Nietzsche was willing to make none. We might say with the critic Erich Heller that in Rilke's story "Der Apostel," the *Visions*, and *Ewald Tragy* "the effects of Nietzsche's hammering and dynamiting are unmistakable; yet there is not the slightest trace of the depth and com-

39

[52]*RMR: Creative Anguish of a Modern Poet*, Princeton, 1956, p. 57 ff. Graff's discussion, though incisive, skirts Rilke's motivation in writing the story.

[53]*Chronicle of a Life*, London: Heinemann, 1953, p. 60.

plexity of Nietzsche's thought and feeling."[54] However, it is just as important to see to what use Rilke turned some of the Nietzschean ideas.

The story of "The Apostle" essentially is simple: A pale, austere stranger sits amid a group of wealthy people who are exhorted to a crusade of charity on behalf of villagers made destitute by a fire; all agree enthusiastically except for the outlandish stranger who launches a tirade against doles, charity, and pity; these, he claims, are forms of bondage and poison which corrode character. The magnanimous Nazarene, says the apostle, or stranger of the story, brought love, a bounty for the strong but only further debilitation for the weak. The notion of love as a poison for the weak is carried through in the *Visions* as are the ideas on passivity, meekness, and blind devotion. What Rilke scores in both the "Apostel" and the *Visions* is the enervating effect of pity and charity as against the strength of the solitary with his individualistic convictions. "The Apostle" can be read as a hymn of hate both against humanity and Christ but this would be putting the accent in the wrong places. The emphasis should be on Rilke's insurrection against charity and pity as reflections of ostentatious self-satisfying impulses of the giver, though well-meaning in the case of Christ. What man needs is self-reliance, the mark of the strong, a belief which Rilke was to reiterate. He adopted Emerson's motto, "The hero is he who is immovably centered," a figure who reappears in Rilke's final elegies. The apostle is possessed of arrogance and towering pride as he lashes out against the condescensions of society. One may note that pride gives the apostle stature and pride gives Christ stature in the *Visions*: it is in moments of immense pride that Christ is arrayed in dignity and most boldly asserts his nobility as well as reveals what otherwise would remain hidden in the recesses of the mind. Of the published story with its hysterical outbursts Rilke said that it was "my half-serious, half-satiric confession of faith." Extravagances in "The Apostle" and in the *Visions* often lead one away from the essential ideas. What all of this does reflect biographically is the smart inflicted on his vanity by his necessary dependence upon family and relatives who, except for his mother, mocked his poetic inspirations and his exuberant desire "to draw moustaches upon the clouds," as he said. That the prophetic apostle was not a static figure but one capable of transformations, like Rilke himself, is evident in the fact that he appeared years later in Rilke's "Prayer" poems as Apostol, an humble and devout monk in search of God; the intervening years marked a progression from extravaganza to thought-out personal ethics. Neither Nietzsche, who declaimed publicly, nor Rilke, who kept his religious thinking fairly private, was able to foretell the irony of the thirties: when once the fabric of German society was torn it was not the overman who emerged but the subhuman. The moralists of the nineteenth century, from Carlyle to Nietzsche, with

[54]Heller, *The Disinherited Mind*, New York: Farrar, Straus & Cudahy, second edition, 1957; Walter Kaufmann, *From Shakespeare to Existentialism*, New York: Doubleday, 1960; and Fritz Dehn, "Rilke und Nietzsche: Ein Versuch," *Euphorion*, 37 (1936), offer substantial discussion of the Nietzsche and Rilke relation.

40

their anti-democratic ideals, unintentionally provide grist for the immoralists of the twentieth century.

Attempts by critics to impute an excess of influence by Nietzsche over Rilke steer a hazardous course between similarities and invention. Rejection of traditions in order to start anew, openness to experience, admiration for antiquity, homelessness, and ecstatic visions Nietzsche and Rilke have in common, but they part ways in attitudes toward the afterlife, women, childhood, the concept of transformation, possessions, the inner landscape, and timelessness as a transcendent reality. Nietzsche's quest embodied the will to power and a somewhat systematized ideology; Rilke's the will to poetry and expression of psychological nuances rather than programmatic teaching.

The *Visions* play an important role in the growth of Rilke's conceptual framework. A year after the *Visions* were written, Rilke told a correspondent of a formidable task which had been everpresent, namely to exorcise "those most terrifying devotional habits of my being, which have since childhood longed to take possession of my poetry." Expulsion of ideas, sentiments, and of habits that had accreted was to be achieved by giving them names and dress and a reality that could be dealt with. In this sense, the *Visions* are a poetic act of exorcism. A stage of rebellion, doubt, and skepticism marked the post-military school days, a stage which was fostered by reading, thinking, and projecting ideas into poetry that could be tested for expression of intent. The flaccidity and falseness of routine or reciprocity-seeking prayer needed to be revalued; the idea of meekness was abandoned in the light of its experienced futility.

Doubts when turned on the objects of belief once cherished can become fierce. So, fired by emotions rooted in private antagonisms and rationalized intellectually, René worked on his visions of Christ. For Rilke Christ was the childhood repository of unanswered prayers, a joyless and disconsolate figure who rejected and denied mortal life and love, the interloper and intruder between himself and his fanatically religious mother—Christ was his mother's other-directed love. Her metaphysically gilded love—especially for the "poor wooden saints"—was to Rilke a distortion of human expression. Intellectually, the figure of Christ as a mediator was unacceptable to Rilke as were the concepts of martyrdom, asceticism, and sin; Rilke strove for an "unmediated" vision to include infinities reaching beyond Christ and Judeo-Christian historiography that postulates a beginning and an end for the world—from creation to the day of judgment. The idea of immortality appealed to Rilke: "I believe that nothing that is real can pass away." Predicating an eternal present, Rilke erased the boundaries between the here and the hereafter and rejected the idea of resurrection. Further, he saw the Christ figure as a captive "bourgeois Christian imitatio," a reflected image of a society which he despised, a pitiful, inconsolable figure who could help neither himself nor others, a figure pointing to the beyond instead of showing how life ought to be lived to the fullest. One of Rilke's first steps in compensating for the loss of faith and in establishing a new

41

certainty through the artist's mission was his hysterical inversion of values as exemplified in his story of the apostle; his aim was to give clear outlines to his own turmoil as well as to shock and unsettle the complacent reader, a kind of bourgeois-baiting found in Baudelaire and which became immensely popular among the *avant garde* of Rilke's day. For Rilke "The Apostle" served as a violent cathartic enabling him a little less than a year later in the *Visions* more stringently to control his materials. In the *Visions*, for the most part, a deliberate and measured tone blends balladistic sentimentality and rhetorical fury.

Aside from the *Visions*, Rilke does not deal ambitiously with Christ themes. "Die Kreuzigung" (1899, "The Crucifixion") pictures Christ's awakening on the cross; finding himself still alive, he invites the Roman captain with his lance to "plant death" in his breast. Already Christ has "weaned" himself from accustomed earthly things and 'droplike quivers on the rim of life.' The sensation of the moment of transition from life to death, without fear, is what Christ wishes to experience. The psychology of that "moment"—to the point of anxiety—continued to intrigue Rilke up to his own death. Of interest is the line in the crucifixion poem, "Sein Wille wahr so sehr entwöhnt [weaned from] der Welt," which previews the one of the first elegy written in 1912, "man entwöhnt sich des Irdischen sanft . . ." Specific speculation on Christ's death changed to a more generalized view of the moment of death but Rilke's basic concern continues thematically through the years.

In "Das Abendmahl" (1903, "The Last Supper"), "the old loneliness steals over" Christ and in "Der Ölbaum-Garten" (1906, "The Garden of Olives") he futilely searches for God but finds himself "alone with mankind's woes/which I tried to assuage with Your help,/ You who do not exist . . ." Another poem, "Kreuzigung" (1908, "Crucifixion"), deals with the spectacle enjoyed by the public and ends with, "Maria screamed, Christ bellowed," which was included in his *New Poems* but certainly does not reach the poetic level of the *Visions*. A few poems in the cycle *Das Marien-Leben* (1913, *The Life of the Virgin Mary*) directly concern Christ, with the suggestion that the vanity of Mary goaded Christ into unwilling demonstration of miracles. Further, according to Rilke, if the savioristic or messianic impulse existed in Christ, it was misdirected because "saviors must be hewn from the granite of mountains." But again, this cycle is no high-water mark for Rilke; it is not devotional in any sense. However, the proximity of the Mary cycle to the first elegy illustrates the symbiotic relation of religious and secular thought in Rilke's poetry.

Rilke's Christ—a figure of silence, a "possessor of all sufferings," standing on his "tower of endurance" as in the poem "Christi Höllenfahrt" (1913, "The Harrowing of Hell")—was to represent a complex interpretation and rendering distinct from what appeared in the literature of Rilke's day. The schools of realism and naturalism contrasted the gentleness of Christ and primitive Christianity to the harsh conditions created by modern technology, pointing to inhospitality of the times to Christ's teachings as well

Rilke a few years after writing the *Visions* (drawing).

as the need for other remedial action. Some even went so far as to score Christ as an oriental figure unsuited to a God concept and Christianity indigenous to Teutonic lands and to the Germanic children of the legendary hero Siegfried.[55] Rilke saw no affinity of such versions of Christ with his own. He made some acid comments on Gerhart Hauptmann's novel *Der Narr in Christo Emanuel Quint* (1910, *The Fool in Christ*), rejecting the quasi-mystical Christ who returns in modern dress to propound human socialism and who attracts the economically oppressed. Although Hauptmann's Christ is distinctly human and is deserted by his followers when the mission becomes hazardous, he does not have sufficient psychological depth; he is a figure of selflessness when compared with the strong self-consciousness and individuality of Rilke's Christ. Privately, during a period of 54 years of what Hauptmann called "my difficult religious wrestlings," he was to come closer to Rilke's conception, although the devotional tenor remained, judging from what was published of *Der Grosse Traum* (*The Great Dream*), poems written in terza rima and inspired in other ways by Dante. A major aspect of these poems is his vision of Christ, reflecting a "lifelong dialogue" with Christ. Unfortunately, Hauptmann willed that the manuscript-book remain at his side "as a companion in the face of eternity," and his wife placed it under his head in his coffin.[56] Although the other side of life, death, was just as real to Rilke, he felt no need to face eternity with anything except mental preparation.

* * *

"To believe what one does not believe does not

exhilarate," said Emily Dickinson, another poet who worked from the center outward. And Rilke felt the same; he could not admit into his poetry belief or content for which he had no enthusiasm. His unbounded poetic imagination could not chain itself to dogma and convention; it had to blossom independently and create its own universe. Many poets have gone through similar crises and have experienced "that old codicil of doubt" that causes beliefs to go down into the dust, recapitulating the larger tension of a time looking back upon a world that is dead and the other "powerless to be born." Familiar too is a poet's founding of a church within by emotional and intellectual avenues: doubt, skepticism, throwing away of childhood prayer, scanning the sky with suspicion, disillusionment, spurning the envoy and seeking God by one's self though he seems to be "a distant—stately Lover."[57]

[55]German naturalism dealt with the Christ figure but much of the literature was third-rate. Because most of it also was published after Rilke had written his own *Visions*, the ties which Marianne Sievers (*Die biblischen Motive in der Dichtung Rainer Maria Rilkes*, Berlin, 1938) attempts to establish may be discounted; comparisons with the works cited by Sievers show more differences than similarities to Rilke's views which transcend the idea of "nation."

[56]K. L. Tank, *Hauptmann in Selbstzeugnissen*, Hamburg: Rowohlt, 1959, p. 148 ff. The most extensive gathering of poems belonging to *Der Grosse Traum* may be found in Gerhart Hauptmann, *Sämtliche Werke*, volume IV, Berlin, Propyläen, 1964, pp. 950-1249.

[57]Emily Dickinson, "God is a distant—stately Lover." The poem wittily scores vicarious courtship of God through Christ. On publication in 1891, it shocked readers and caused one to call it "contemptuous Unitarianism." The *cause célèbre* is described by Thomas H. Johnson, editor, *The Poems of Emily Dickinson*, volume I, Cambridge: Harvard University Press, 1955, pp. 284-85.

44

To what extent Rilke reconstituted the mytho-poetic content of Christianity in fashioning the poetry of his *Visions* may be seen in his eclectic dealings with the Gospels. Attracted primarily to St. Luke (particularly the homilies and sermons) because Luke was more interested in the character of Christ than was the doctrinaire St. Matthew, Rilke too maintains an individual point-of-view of Christ, as we have seen. Yet, of the two different versions of Christ on the cross, Rilke chose the disillusioned words of Matthew rather than Luke's version of a gracious acceptance of destiny. Further, in the *Visions* Rilke gave Christ composite characteristics and a range of emotional capacities that created a figure in the round and certainly sounded greater depths than any of the nineteenth century German, French, English, and American poetry dealing with Christ. In the *Visions* we hear echoes of Swinburne who, in translation, was on Rilke's reading list: "Thou hast conquered, O pale Galilean; the world has grown gray from thy breath;/ We have drunken of things Lethean, and fed on the fullness of death;"[58] we also see touches of Hugo and the French romanticists who characterize Christ, the immensely lonely one like the artist, as a romantic hero, the *grand homme foudroyé*—the thunderer. Rilke touches these as well as other facets in his interpretation of the historical Christ—the man of sorrow, of disillusionment, the carrier of a message and mission which was misinterpreted and distorted by followers, the king of children, a man despised and venerated, a man of the senses and the spirit who was caught up in the conflict between these dualities, a man of melancholia and noble pride, a man of strength and helplessness. In short, Rilke saw in the solitary genius of Christ a complex person toward whom he displayed antipathy in the role of mediator and implied divinity, but sympathy whenever he equated Christ's lot and human suffering with that of the artist. These ambivalent emotions evident in the *Visions* should make clear the falsity of critics' oversimplified characterizations of Rilke as an Antichrist. It would not be amiss to compare, for example, the deep inner compulsion of Rilke to make his case with the experience of Albert Schweitzer. A close reading of the New Testament can yield the conclusion that the historical Jesus was not the "gentle Jesus, meek and mild" of childhood hymns but an apocalyptically minded person in the tradition of the prophets, as Rilke portrayed him in some of the *Vision* poems. Schweitzer presented Christ as expecting the end of the world momentarily and believing appointment by God to rule the coming supernatural kingdom. Schweitzer fostered a profound trend in twentieth century re-evaluations,

> Even if liberal Christianity has to give up identifying its belief with the teachings of Jesus in the way it used to think possible, it still has the spirit of Jesus not against it but on its side. Jesus no doubt fits his teachings into the late Messianic dogma, but he does not think dogmatically. He formulates no doctrine. He is far from judging any man's belief by reference to any standard of dogmatic correctness. Nowhere does he demand of his hearers that they shall sacrifice thinking to believing. Quite the contrary! He bids them meditate upon religion. In the Sermon on the Mount he lets

[58]"Hymn to Proserpine" (1860).

45

ethics, as the essence of religion, flood their hearts, leading them to judge the value of piety by what it makes of a man from the ethical point of view.[59]

Rilke would agree that the historical Christ and the one of tradition were different, that ethics and not dogma constitute the heart of religion; particularly he stressed the significance of the Sermon on the Mount.

Further, Rilke suggested that the teachings of Christ have been misunderstood in the modern world. Much of his work subsequent to the *Visions* was devoted to thinking out poetically the implication of the ethics of love, the essence of prayer, the meaning of God, the destiny of man in the cosmos, and such corollaries as the question of immortality. A wood and leather-bound Lutheran Bible dated 1770, which included the Old and New Testament and the Apocrypha, was a companion everpresent in Rilke's life.

Belief is valid only on its own terms; it is neither false—for which some critics have taken Rilke to task —nor true in a verifiable sense. Belief is the axiom of emotion. But Rilke went one step further and called for dispensing with "belief" in favor of "feeling," defining religion as a direction of the heart as did Pascal. Rilke noted that his relation to God "is not to be characterized as denominational." His was a personal search for the meaning of existence and a desire to establish a relationship with, if not dependence upon, powers above man. As the noted novelist Robert Musil, an alumnus of Rilke's military school, said in a memorial address: "He was in a definite sense the most religious poet since Novalis but I am

46

not at all sure that he had religion. He saw things differently—in a new intuitive way." In the *Visions*, Rilke rejected Christ's assertion: "no man cometh unto the Father, but by me" (St. John, 14:6). With variations, Rilke called for an immediacy of experience: "Whoever is compelled by inward religious necessity, he already has established for himself a relation with God, which transcends nation and church."[60] The similarity between Rilke's belief—in this respect—and that of the Antinomians and Quakers is striking. And, in the course of correspondence with a Protestant pastor during 1922, he wrote: "Personally closer to me are all those religions in which the mediator is minimally present or totally absent." During this correspondence, Rilke made his position towards Christianity clear: "Seen from the perspective of old origins, the Christian position, the great Christian event, will always appear as one of the most marvelous attempts to keep the way open to God."[61] Other avenues to God he saw in the worship by the people of antiquity—the old Egyptians and particularly the Greeks with their emphasis on

[59]Albert Schweitzer, *The Psychiatric Study of Jesus: Exposition and Criticism,* translated by C. R. Joy, Boston: Beacon Press, 1963, p. 25.

[60]Translated from a little-known essay which Rilke contributed to a symposium: *Die Lösung der Judenfrage,* edited by Julius Moses, Berlin: Wigand, 1907, p. 192. Also, SW VI, pp. 1003-05.

[61]Between February 1921 and March 1922, Rilke wrote about five letters to Pastor Rudolf Zimmermann in which the concept of religiosity is clarified. Rilke more than hints that he prefers his ideas to come to life in poetry rather than concretize them in evanescent prose.

physicality and the here-and-now—and in the close man-God relationship of the Mosaic and Mohammedan religions. Like Yeats, Rilke did not view Christianity as a satisfactory religion and thought Protestant ritual to be cold and Catholic to be too dogmatic. Yet Rilke and Yeats created some splendid and objective Biblical *personae* in their poetry.[62] Esthetic appreciation of the symbology of religions and the Christian calendar of religious days found expression in his works and in such personal habits as wearing a Russian cross; but his religious sensibility was original and without commitment to any creed.

The *Visions* helped Rilke to chart his way into the open. While writing the poems he had briefly gone to Italy and admired the artists of the Renaissance, but at the same time he felt that they had been only in their "spring season," caught and arrested by their religious orientation, rather than experiencing a full blossoming into summer ripeness. In the same way, the *Visions* were Rilke's springtime whose efforts belong, as he noted in a diary entry of 1898, to "honest and sincere work, yes, perhaps one's most honest." With mutations, the ideas formed in the *Visions* branch into later poetry which he called "the undatable works:" *The Book of Hours, Sonnets to Orpheus, Duino Elegies.*[63] In the *Visions* Rilke detached himself from any creed and cant while in the other works he alternately saw God as the object of love which the monk Apostol tried to grasp through mystical contact, God as immanent in nature (the sonnets), and final reconciliation in the elegies with

the idea that the angel—not to speak of the divine—is disdainful and unapproachable, throwing man back upon his own spiritual resources and own search for fulfillment. Rilke's ideas in these poetic works strike a ready chord in the modern (yet old) religious currents of our sixties, namely that God, or Christ, or any deity is dead unless he has a vital and personal meaning for each individual. Rilke believed that when the individual comes to accept the idea that religion cannot give "consolation" to humans, though it mistakenly tries, only at that point can "a unique religious productivity take place, leading not to consolation but to a decisive ability to do without consolation."[64] In the *Visions*, the hands of Christ, those of the nun, the Church of Nago, and the heavens are symbolically empty.

Some of the early ideals for the writing of poetry, which Rilke held before him in writing the *Visions*, are expressed in an essay of 1893 called *The Wanderer*,[65] an analysis of Goethean techniques. Rilke noted that the poet must create a picture upon whose shimmering details and life drama the reader can feast his eyes and mind. It is necessary for the poet not only to capture the world as he sees it but also "to

47

[62]How Yeats' views were translated into poetry is best described by Curtis Bradford, *Yeats at Work.* Carbondale: Southern Illinois University Press, 1965.

[63]Mövius, *RMR*, p. 152, obtained this statement in conversation with Lou Andreas-Salomè. In a letter to Zimmermann (February 3, 1921), Rilke assigns the *Stunden-Buch* to his juvenilia but calls it, nevertheless, "undatable."

[64]Letter to Zimmermann, February 3, 1921.

[65]SW V, pp. 283-87.

create a world for himself as others see it." Possessing the gift of imagination, the poet "carries worlds within him and is ever rich." A longing for antiquity leads the poet's emotions back to themes rooted in the past. Beyond these elements, the poet's figures have symbolic meanings. Some of the poetic modes observed in Goethe, Rilke applied to the *Visions*: balladistic and narrative detail couched in drama, only infrequently found in his later poetry; an imaginative re-creation and interpretation of Christ, the wanderer, from different vantage points—including Christ's; and the universality of characters who are symbols as well as individuals, restless, inquisitive, searching—prototypes of the poet and the human spirit. Evidently then, the young Rilke's artistic intent and ideological struggle are embodied in the *Visions*.

At the time Rilke still was occupied with the *Visions*, he wrote to a friend that the Christ cycle "emphasizes the other side of my lyricism which has appeared perhaps monotonously timid in my volumes of poetry published hitherto."[66] It is the other side of Rilke which appears in the *Visions*, a little-known side that Rilke for a variety of reasons—justifiably or not—wished to keep hidden until the time was ripe for their publication. In the case of a great poet particularly, more is lost than gained by keeping any work hidden. The time for the publication of Rilke's *Visions* was long overdue. Now indeed, the eleven poems of the cycle add not only to an understanding of his formative years but also to clarification of the basic "personal religiosity," as Rilke put it, that was transformed into the inner dynamics of his subsequent poetry.

—S.M.

[66]Quoted by Sievers, p. 80, from an unpublished letter in the Rilke Archives.

Notes

The German text of Rilke's *Christus: Elf Visionen* (1896/1898) appears in volume III, *Rainer Maria Rilke: Sämtliche Werke*, Insel-Verlag. References to the *Sämtliche Werke* is indicated by SW: volume I, 1955, includes all previously published major and minor poetic works; volume II, 1957, contains Rilke's French poems as well as posthumous German poems from 1906-1926; volume III, 1959, has poems from 1884-1905, including first versions and previously unpublished poems like the *Visions of Christ* cycle; volume IV, 1961, has Rilke's short stories, sketches, and plays; volume V, 1965, includes monographs on art, essays, and reviews from 1893-1905; volume VI includes prose works, poems in prose, and other writings from 1906-1926, published in 1966.

Indispensable for an understanding of Rilke's childhood and Prague years are the following works which however are not in complete agreement about interpreting biographical events: *Briefe, Verse und Prosa aus dem Jahre 1896*, ed. Richard von Mises, with an introduction, New York: Johannespresse, 1946; *Briefe an Baronesse von Oe*, ed. Richard von Mises, with an introduction, New York: Johannespresse, 1945; Peter Demetz, *René Rilkes Prager Jahre*, Düsseldorf: Diederichs, 1953; Carl Sieber, *René Rilke: Die Jugend Rainer Maria Rilkes*, Leipzig: Insel-Verlag, 1932; *Rilkes Leben und Werk im Bild*, ed. Ingeborg Schnack, with an introduction by J. R. von Salis, Wiesbaden: Insel-Verlag, 1956; *Kafka and Prague*, text by Emanuel Frynta, photographs by Jan Lukas, Prague: Artia, 1960.

Of the collections of Rilke letters, the most accessible to English readers are *Letters of Rainer Maria Rilke*, translated by J. B. Greene and M. D. H. Norton, volume I, 1892-1910, volume II, 1910-1926, New York: Norton, 1945, 1947; *Selected Letters of Rainer Maria Rilke*, ed. Harry T. Moore, New York: Doubleday, 1960. The dates and the names of correspondents identify the letters in the various German or English collections.

49

Rainer Maria Rilke: VISIONS of CHRIST

1896-1898

Christus: Elf Visionen / Visions of Christ

Christus: Elf Visionen / Visions of Christ

[Titled by Ernst Zinn, editor of *Sämtliche Werke*.]

DIE WAISE

Sie trollten sich. Es war ein schlecht Begängnis,—
die letzte Klasse. Keine Glocke klang.
Die Kleine sann: Lang war die Muttter krank,
durch Jahre war die Stube ihr Gefängnis.
Sie sagten Alle heute: Gott sei Dank—
sie ist erlöst. —Ihr aber war so bang
vor einem unerklärlichen Verhängnis.
Ja, und was jetzt? Sie haben sie verscharrt.
Du lieber Gott, was ist doch gar so hart
der feuchte Hügel da von Schutt und Steinen.
Und Mütterchen war doch gewohnt an Leinen
als weiches Lager. Und ihr kommt ein Weinen.
Warum sie sie so schlecht gebettet haben?
Warum in dumpfe, schwarze Erde graben
was hoch im Himmel helle Heimat hat?—
Der Himmel! Das muß eine Märchenstadt
mit goldnen Kuppeln sein and weißen Gassen,
dort ist nur Licht und Liebe—nicht zu fassen,
und niemand ist dort traurig und verlassen,
und selig Singen ist dort alles Tun.
Ein Stern ist Spielzeug wie das weiße Schaf,
mit dem die Kleine wohl zu spielen traf,
und ist dort oben eins besonders brav,
darfs in des Mondes Silberwiege ruhn,
verkrochen in der Wolken Flockenflaum.
Das muß ein Schlaf dort sein—und erst ein Traum!

THE ORPHAN

They shuffled after. It was sad to see—
the cheapest rites: no tolling of a bell.
The youngster mused: mother had not been well;
for years the room had been her dungeon-cell.
Today they all remarked: Thank God—she's free.—
It was so fearsome, though, to face alone
a destiny mysterious and unknown.
Yes, and what now? They've put her in the ground.
Dear God in Heaven, why should this damp mound
of rubbish and of rubble press so hard?
Mother has, after all, been used to sleeping
on linen. And she does deserve some weeping.
Why have they bedded her without regard?
Why bury someone in the dank, black loam
who, high in heaven, has a radiant home?
Heaven! that story-town, where every dome
is made of gold, and every street is white;
nothing is there but lots of love and light—
and no one's gloomy and forsaken there,
and blissful singing is the whole affair.
A star, there, is a toy—like the white sheep
with which the little girl once loved to leap;
and were she truly good, she'd be allowed
to cradle in the moon's own silver beam,
burrowing deep inside a downy cloud.
That must be quite a sleep—and quite a dream!

53

Da sieht die Kleine aus dem Sinnen auf:
Der Frühling wartet rings mit tausend Blüten,
und wie in jenen tiefen Märchenmythen,
drin braune Zwerge rote Schätze hüten,
ist lauter eitel Gold der Kirchturmknauf.
Nein, ist die Gotteswelt doch eine Pracht
und neu, als hätt der Herr sie just gemacht;
der Kleinen ists ein Jubel—und sie lacht.
Da schaut sie: drüben an der Kirchhofmauer
lehnt noch ein Mann so reglos und so müd;
in seinem dunkelgroßen Auge glüht
wie eine trübe Totenkerze—Trauer.
Derb ist und bäuerisch sein grau Gewand;
ins wirre Haar krallt er die irre Hand
und starrt verloren nach der Berge Rand
als ob zum Fluge in das fremde Land
sich seiner Seele leise Schwinge breite.

Die Kleine trippelt kindisch ihm zur Seite
und staunt ihn groß mit Frageaugen an
und dann klingts alltagsfremd und unverdorben:
"Du, was bist du so traurig, fremder Mann,—
ist dir vielleicht auch Mütterchen gestorben?"
Er hört es nicht. Sein fremdes Auge sinnt
noch immer Wunder, und er sagt nur leise
ungern gestört wie der verlorne Weise
dem sich ein Neues drängt in Kraft und Kreise:
"Geh heim zu deiner Mutter, Kind."

The child looks up, and leaves her thoughts behind:
Spring waits for her with flowers of every kind;
and as it is in that mysterious story
of red hoards guarded by the brown dwarf-people,
there is real gold atop the prayer-house steeple.
God's universe is, after all, a glory—
and new, as if He'd made it overnight.
The child rejoices—and she laughs outright.
But look: stock-still against the churchyard wall,
a man who seems to have no strength at all
is leaning; in his great, dark eyes are fed
the fires of grief, like candles for the dead.
Rustic his clothing, of a coarse gray thread;
he claws his wild hair with a wandering hand
and stares, quite lost, toward the mountain's rand
as if with pinions quietly outspread
his spirit readies for that other land.

Childishly she comes skipping alongside
and gapes at him with eyes grown question-wide;
and innocently then her words ring out:
"You, stranger, what are you so sad about,—
is it because your mother, too, has died?"
He doesn't hear. With eye still fixed intently
on miracles, he merely murmurs gently,
vexed to have been disturbed—like a sage brooding,
upon whose sphere an upstart is intruding:
"Go home to mother; go, my dear."

Fritz von Uhde's painting *Die Jünger von
Emmaus* (detail), *The Disciples of Emmaus*, 1885.

Da schrickt das Kind zusammen: "Du, ich habe
dir doch gesagt, ich hab nicht Mutter mehr."
"So," nickt der Fremde dumpf, "ist sie im Grabe?"
Er senkt die Hand aufs Haupt des Kindes schwer
und träumt den Segen: Leicht sei ihr die Erde.

Da ist der Kleinen wieder bang. Ihr nagts
am Herzen wieder wie ein wildes Weh,
sie schmiegt sich näher in des Grauen Näh:
"Nichtwahr, du weißt es auch, im Himmel seh
ich wieder sie—nichtwahr—der Pfarrer sagts?"
Das Wort verweht, ein leises Heimchen geigt,
die Kleine horcht, ein weißer Falter reigt,
die Kleine horcht, aus fernen Hütten steigt
ein Zitterrauch . . . Der große Graue schweigt.

At this the child recoils: "You didn't hear?
I said I've lost her." "So," a stolid nod,
"She's buried?" On the young one's brow he lays
a heavy hand, and in a trance he prays:
Lightly upon your mother lie the sod!

The child is fearful, as she was before.
A savage grief gnaws at her heart once more;
she sidles closer to the man in gray:
"Isn't it so—the priest says she and I—
you know it too—will meet in heaven some day?"
Her words drift off; there comes a cricket-cry;
she harks; a dainty whiteness flutters by;
she harks; a shudder of smoke ascends the sky
from distant huts . . . The man makes no reply.

❖ ❖ ❖

❖ ❖ ❖

JUDENFRIEDHOF

Ein Maienabend. —Und der Himmel flittert
vor lauter Lichte. Seine Marken glühn.
Die grauen Gräbersteine, moosverwittert,
deckt jetzt der Frühling mit dem besten Blühn;
so legt die Waise—und ihr Händchen zittert—
auf Mutters totes Antlitz junges Grün.

Hier dringt kein Laut her von der Straße Mühn,
fernab verlieren sich die Tramwaygleise,
und auf den weißen Wegen wandelt leise
ins rote Sterben träumerisch der Tag.
Der alte Judenfriedhof ists in Prag.
Und Dämmer sinkt ins winklige Gehöf,
drin Spiro schläft, der Held im Schlachtenschlagen,
und mancher weise Mann, von dem sie sagen,
daß zu der Sonne ihn sein Flug getragen,
voran der greise hohe Rabbi Löw,
um den noch heut verwaiste Jünger klagen.—

Jetzt wird ein Licht wach in des Torwarts Bude,
aus deren schlichtem Eisenschlote raucht
ein karges Mahl. —Bei Liwas Grabe taucht
jetzt langsam Jesus auf. Der arme Jude,
nicht der Erlöser, lächelnd und erlaucht.
Sein Aug ist voll von tausend Schmerzensnächten,
und seine schmale blasse Lippe haucht:
"Jehovah—weh, wie hast du mich mißbraucht,
hier wo der treuste ruht von deinen Knechten,
hier will ich, greiser Gott, jetzt mit dir rechten!—

JEWISH CEMETERY

A Maynight.—Brilliant lights are splashed across
the sky. Its markers glow. The gray old stones,
disintegrating in the grip of moss,
Spring now bedecks with the best flowers she owns;
so—her hand trembling—does an orphan place
young verdure on her mother's death-gray face.

No hint of the street's hardship reaches here;
far off the tracks of tramways disappear;
along the white roads, in a reverie,
toward its red death the day walks quietly.
It's Prague's old Jewish graveyard. And the light
is sinking in these crooked lanes, where Spiro
lies slumbering, the golden warrior-hero,
alongside many wise men whose bold flight
transported them, it's said, unto the sun,
led by old Rabbi Löw, the lustrous one
mourned even now by followers of his truth.—

A light awakens in the gateway booth,
out of whose iron chimney, sleek and smooth,
a scanty meal smokes forth. At Liwa's grave
Jesus emerges slowly. The poor Jew—
not the redeemer, smiling and most brave.
Within his eye are thousand nights of rue;
from thin, pale lips a bit of breath comes through:
"How badly I've been treated, Lord, by you!
Here where he rests, your most devoted slave,
here, graybeard God, we'll settle scores, we two.

Denn um mit dir zu kämpfen kam ich her.
Wer hat dir Alles denn gegeben, wer?—
Der Alten Lehre hatte mancher Speer
aus Feindeshand ein blutend Mal geschlagen,—
da brachte ich mein Glauben und mein Wagen,
da ließ ich neu dein stolzes Gottbild ragen
und gab ihm neue Züge, rein und hehr.
Und in der Menschen irres Wahngewimmel
warf deinen Namen ich—das große 'Er'.
Und dann von tausend Erdensorgen schwer
stieg meine Seele in den hohen Himmel,
und meine Seele fror; denn er war *leer*.
So warst du niemals—oder warst nicht mehr,
als ich Unsel'ger auf die Erde kam.
Was kümmerte mich auch der Menschheit Gram,
wenn du, der Gott, die Menschen nicht mehr scharst
um deinen Thron. —Wenn gläubiges Gefleh
nur Irrsinn ist, du nie dich offenbarst,
weil du nicht bist.—Einst wähnt' ich, ich gesteh,
ich sei (die) Stimme deiner Weltidee. . . .
Mein Alles war mir, Vater, deine Näh . . .
Du Grausamer, und wenn du niemals warst,
so hätte meine Liebe und mein Weh
dich schaffen müssen bei Gethsemane."

· · · · · · · · · · · · · · · · · · · ·

58

For I have come to fight you here. Who gave
everything that is yours to boast of, who?—
Many a bloody mark the foeman drew
upon your creed with swords that slashed and slew,—
but then I brought my faith, my daring too,
and let your godhood glory forth anew,
and gave it a new face, sublime and true.
And when mankind in frenzied mobs would rave,
your name—the great *"He"*—unto them I threw.
And then my soul, heavy with human care,
took wing, and up to highest heaven it flew;
and my soul froze, because the place was *bare*.
So you had never been—or were no more
when I, poor wretch, set foot upon this shore.
Why should the grief of men be my affair,
when you, the great God, summon them before
your throne no longer? when their pious prayer
is only madness—since you'll not reveal
your face, because you're not.—There came to me
a dream one day, that I was born to be
the voice of your idea, your sign and seal . . .
My one wish, sire, was closeness unto thee . . .
Terrible one, and since you were not real,
it was my love, it was my agony
that gave you being at Gethsemane."

The tombstone of Rabbi Löw.

Im Wärterhäuschen ist das Licht verlöscht.
Und in dem Bett von Gräbern breit umböscht
fließt schon des blauen Mondquells Wunderwelle.
Und Sterne schaun mit Kinderaugenhelle
verstohlen über schwarzen Giebelrand.—

Und Christus, zu des Rabbi Gruft gewandt:
"Dir auch gefiel es, Alter, manchen Spruch
zur Ehre jenes Gotts zusammzuschweißen.
Wer hat dich, morscher Tor, auch blättern heißen
in alten Psalmen und im Bibelbuch?
Du hast so viel gewußt, stehst im Geruch,
dich gar geheimer Weisheit zu befleißen.
Heraus damit jetzt! Weißt du keinen Fluch,
daß ich des Himmels blaues Lügentuch
mit seiner Schneide kann in Stücke reißen.
Hast du kein Feuer in den Dämmerungen
des Alchymistenherdes je entdeckt,
das fürchterlich und ewig unbezwungen
mit gierem Lecken seine Rachezungen
bis zu des Weltalls fernen Angel(n) streckt?
Kennst du kein Gift, das süß ist wie der Kuß
der Mutter, das nach seligem Genuß
den Ahnungslosen sicher töten muß.
O Glück, die ganze Welt so zu vergiften.
Weißt du kein Mittel, herben Haß zu stiften,
der jeden Mann zum wilden Raubtier macht?

60

The light in the attendant's hut goes dim.
And down the broad-sloped bed of tombs there course
marvelous billows from the moon's blue source.
And stars, like eyes aglow with childish whim,
peek slyly over the black gable's rim.—

Christ turns to Löw's crypt, and addresses him:
"It pleased you, too, to patch together verse,
old man, in honor of that God of yours.
Who made you leaf the Bible, foolish corse,
and scrutinize old psalters, hymn by hymn?
You knew so much; and still you studied, earning
a reputation for much occult learning.
Out with it now! Is there no malediction
so sharp that I can shear each lying section—
aye, cut to shreds heaven's blue cloth of fiction?
In alchemy's old hearths, can there be burning
no fire, engendered by a special curse,
fierce and unquenchable, forever turning
its vengeful tongues to lick without remorse
the utmost hinges of the universe?
Is there no poison, sweet as mother's kiss,
which, after lifting him to happiness,
murders the unsuspecting in his bliss?
What joy, to poison the whole world with this!
Have you no means for bringing hate to birth,
that turns each man into a beast of prey?

Kannst du nicht ziehn in diese stillen Triften
die Schauerschrecken einer Völkerschlacht.
Kannst du nicht eine neue Lehre stiften,
die Wahnsinnswut in jeder Brust entfacht.
Ins Unbegrenzte steigre ihre Triebe
und sende Pest und sende Seuchenschwärme,
daß in des Lotterbettes feiler Wärme
die ganze Welt zugrund geht an der Liebe!"

Jach lacht er Hohn. Und in den stummen Steinen
gellts wie des wunden Wildes Sterbeschrei.
Es legt ein Reif sich auf den nächtgen Mai.
Ein schwarzer Falter zieht im Flug vorbei
und er sieht Christum einsam knien und weinen.

Can you not change the pastures of this earth
into a mire of universal fray?
Is there no doctrine you can summon forth,
till every heart's on fire, and wrath holds sway?
Let it sprout high! let nothing hold it back!
Send plague abroad, and let contagions spread,
till in the venal warmth of the slut's bed
Love brings the world to ruin and to rack!"

His laugh is scorn. And where the mute stones lie,
it pierces like a wounded deer's death cry.
A hoarfrost shrouds the Maynight by degrees.
A thing of blackness flutters by, and sees
Christ weeping there alone upon his knees.

61

JAHRMARKT

Das war in München beim Oktoberfeste,
da die Theresienwiese voll vom Schrein
und Schwall der Schauer ist. Da bunte Gäste
aus der Provinz der Kunst der Rindermäste
verständnisvoll ein Mundvoll Worte leihn.
Die kleinen Mädchen, flüchtig ihrem Neste,
durchschwirren keck den lauten Tag zu zwein,
und Bursche mit der bunten Lodenweste
und ziere Stadtherrn bengeln hinterdrein.
Dazwischen drängen Wagen und betreßte
urdumme Kutscher, blinzelnde Lakein,
Fuhrleute dann, die ihre längstgenäßte
gepichte Kehle tüchtig spülen. Kein
Verdroßner stört, und allen schiens das Beste,
daß man sich prall und gar so prächtig preßte
durch diese bauernbunten Budenreihn.
Bier gabs und Wein in Strömen allerorten,
und viel Verständge prüften dran; es ließ
die Blume gelten der und der die Borten.
Marktschreier prahlten an den Bretterpforten
und priesen ihre Wunder weit mit Worten,
als wären sie mit Noah und Konsorten
zurückgekehrt ins echte Paradies.—
An kleinern Ständen bot man Trauben, Torten
und Würste aus; geduldige Hühner schmorten
sich einen goldnen Panzer an am Spieß.

62

THE FAIR

It was at the October festival
of Munich, when Theresa-field is pressed
by onlookers: a screaming, heaving swell.
Provincial folk, whose pleasure is to tell
of making cattle plump, converse and jest.
The little girls, who've somehow fled the nest,
flit boldly through the raucous day in pairs,
pursued by youths in flashy-colored vest
while city-dandies flaunt their phony airs.
Carriages wedge their way, with drivers dressed
in sparkling lace, moronic servingmen
whose passengers, long dry, refuse to rest
until their gullets have been washed again.
No frown disturbs them; all believe it best
to squeeze and shove magnificently past
among these rustic-colored rows of stalls.
Varieties of beer, and waterfalls
of wine, were poured and passed the experts' test;
one paid in flowers, one in bits of lace.
Each barker boasted, with a solemn face,
his wonders were more grand than could be guessed—
as if, along with Noah and his race,
they had returned to man's first bower of grace.
Grapes, tarts, and wursts at smaller stands were sold;
turned on a spit, the patient hens (though hot)
beamed proudly in their armor-plates of gold.

Und drüben stand bewehrt ein schwarzer Tell,
ein Wilder, und vergaß das Schreienmüssen
vor lauter Gieren nach den Kokosnüssen.
Da schob ein Zwerg, ein drolliger Gesell,
mit Grinsemiene sich vorüber, schnell
war dort die ganze Menge hingerissen
zur Wellenschaukel und zum Karussell.
Und wo sie eine rote Fahne hissen,
dort reißt auf grellverhangenem Gestell
dummdreiste Witze der Polichinell.
Die große Trommel hat er durchgeschlissen
und trommelt jetzt trotz tausend Hindernissen
mit seinem unverschämten wilden Wissen
dem lieben Publikum das Trommelfell.

Laut lachend ließ gefallen sichs ein jeder.

Auch ich ging ziellos durch das Weggeäder
und blinzte müßig in das volle Licht,
und manchmal fuhr ich wie so mancher Wicht
der Schönen, die just kam, ins Angesicht
mit meiner kühnen, kecken Pfauenfeder.
Und hinterher konnt' noch ein Silberkichern
von blütenfrischen Lippen mir versichern:
die liebe Kleine grollte nicht. —
Dann gabs ein Ängsten, wenn wo Fässerfuhren
mit plumpen Pferden furchten wegentlang:
Die Menge drängte in die Räderspuren,

And yonder, as if rooted to the spot,
a black man stood who should have bellowed, but
became enraptured of a coconut.
A pigmy, a queer fellow, then pushed by
with strange grimaces, and the crowd forgot
all else, ran off with an enchanted cry
to give the swing and carousel a try.
Wherever a red flag was hoisted high,
there, from a dazzling-curtained platform, spoke
some Punchinello, sharing a sharp joke.
He'd beat the great drum till it all but broke;
and now, despite a thousand handicaps,
with shameless, elemental craft, he taps
a frenzied serenade to these "dear folk."

Each listener laughs aloud, and warmly claps.

I, too, went wandering where my footstep fell,
and idly blinked against the blinding light,
and more than once, like many other chaps,
collided with a late-arriving belle—
my peacock-feather thrust upon her sight.
And afterward a giggling—silver-bright—
of rose-fresh lips assured me all was well:
the darling creature nursed no spite.—
Along came clumsy horses, with a load
of barrels, causing panic on the road:
over the wheel-tracks wildly pressed the throng;

63

München.
Gesamtansicht vom Oktoberfest.

Overview of the Munich October-Fair grounds at the turn of the century.

da schrie ein Kind, ein Bursche sang, da sprang
ein Mädel, dem entfernter Walzertouren
ersehnter Zauber in die Beine drang.
Und was nur immer klingen konnte, klang,
vom Waldhornsolo bis zum Bumerang
dort vor den Buden mit den Wachsfiguren.
Wie ich mich so durch das Getümmel wand,
da stand ich plötzlich an der Wiese Rand
vor einer Bude. Überm Eingang stand
in kargen Lettern zaghaft und bescheiden:
'Das Leben Jesu Christi und sein Leiden.'
Und—ich weiß nicht warum, ich trat hinein.
Schon hielt ich in der Hand den blauen Schein,
der für zehn Pfennig Einlaß mir gewährte.
Ich fragte mich, was den Besitzer nährte;
denn in der Bude war ich ganz allein.

Wer mochte *dem* auch hier sein Denken weihn,
dem Mann, von dem der Katechet ihm lehrte,
daß Buße er gepredigt und Kastein
und daß ein großes Leiden ihn verzehrte.

Da sah ich nun des heilgen Kinds Geburt
und dann die Flucht, da Josef durch die Furt
des Flusses lenkt das Maultier mit Marien,
den Tempel dann, drin ob der Theorien
des Knaben mancher Pharisäer murrt,
und dann den Einzug in Jerusalem,

a youngster shrieked, a boy struck up a song,
a girl waltzed forth, as if some distant goad
bewitched her limbs that had been waiting long.
Whatever had a sound to offer, sounded,
from bugle solo to the drum that pounded
before the little stand—the waxwork stand.
Through the commotion I had somehow floundered
and suddenly was at the meadow's rand
outside a stall. Above the door I spied
lettered in rather timid, modest fashion:
"The story of Christ Jesus and His passion."
And—I don't know just why—I went inside.
The blue slip was already in my hand
to prove that I had paid the ten-cent fee.
Small profit this concession reaped! I scanned
the booth in wonder: no one there but me.

At such a fair who'd waste a single thought
on *him*, who preached of penitence and taught
atonement and himself to grief was brought
—devoured by his own great agony?

I saw the Christ child's birth in Bethlehem;
then Joseph's fording of the stream with them—
leading his wife and babe to liberty;
the temple's next, where many a Pharisee
growls at the lad who dares to disagree;
and then the entrance to Jerusalem,

65

wo er,—zu fragen meidet er, bei wem—
bei schlichten Leuten unter Sünden wohnt
und jeden Willen reich mit Wundern lohnt.
Dann jener Tag, da er sein *deo natus*
dem Volk entgegenschleudert, und Pilatus
sogar den Richtern Milde rät,
bis, weil das Volk zu sänftigen zu spät,
des Bleichen dornbekränzte Majestät
schmerzedel auf der Balustrade steht,
daß Mitleid selbst des Römers Herz durchweht
und er verwirrt sein *"Ecce homo"* fleht. . . .
Umsonst. Es brüllt der Pöbel ungestüm:
Ans Kreuz mit ihm!

Dann kamen alle Greuel jenes Tags,
da er, verurteilt von des Reichs Verwesern,
ans Holz geheftet wurde wilden Schlags:
Nacht brach herein, und in den Wolken lags
wie Racherufe von Posaunenbläsern,
und fremde Vögel gierten nach den Äsern,
und statt des Taus war Blut an allen Gräsern.—

Jetzt starrten beide Schächer hier so gläsern
mich an; es glänzte ihrer Stirnen Wachs.—
Doch Christi Auge, klufttief, todesdunkel,
erlohte in so täuschendem Gefunkel,
daß alles Blut mir heiß zum Herzen schoß:
Der gelbe Wachsgott öffnete und schloß

where—never questioning what they may be—
he lives with poor, plain sinners, and he fills
their days with treasure through his miracles;
then hurls his *deo natus* in the teeth
of orthodoxy—even Pilate's will
is for a gentle judgment; till,
because the populace must have its kill,
the pale one—regal in a thorny wreath—
stands woe-resplendent on the balustrade,
at sight of whom the Roman's heart is swayed
and *ecce homo* weakly he implores . . .
In vain. The mob will not be disobeyed.
"Nail him!" it roars.

The horrors of that day were then portrayed,
when, doomed by the imperial governors,
wildly the man was hammered to the wood:
then came the night, and in the clouded skies
trombones were blowing like avengers' cries,
and strange birds hovered in the neighborhood,
and on the grasses hung not dew, but blood.

Both robbers glared at me with glassy eyes;
their foreheads glowed as waxen foreheads should—
and yet the eyes of Christ: gulf-deep, death-dark,
held such an eerie—almost living—spark,
that all my blood rushed hotly toward my heart:
the eyelids of the waxen God had been

66

das Lid, das, bläulich dünn, den Blick verhängte;
der enge, wunde Brustkorb hob und senkte
sich leise, leise, und die schwammgetränkte,
todblasse Lippe schien ein Wort zu fassen,
das sehnend sich durch starre Zähne drängte:
"Mein Gott, mein Gott—was hast du mich verlassen?"
Und wie ich zu entsetzt, daß ich des Sinns
des dunkeltiefen Dulderworts verstände,
nur steh und steh und nicht das Auge wende,—
da lösen leise seine weißen Hände
sich von dem Kreuze, und er stöhnt: "Ich bins."
Lang lausch ich nach, und es verklingt sein Spruch,—
ich schau die Wände rings von grellem Tuch
bedeckt und fühle diesen Jahrmarktstrug
mit seinem Lampenöl- und Wachsgeruch.
Da haucht es wieder her: Das ist mein Fluch.
Seit mich, von ihrem eitlen Glaubensprahlen
betört, die Jünger aus dem Grabe stahlen,
giebts keine Grube mehr, die mich behält.
Solang aus Bächen Sterne widerstrahlen,
solang die Sonne zu erlösten Talen
den Frühling ruft mit seinen Bacchanalen,
so lange muß ich weiter durch die Welt.
Von Kreuz zu Kreuze muß ich Buße zahlen:
wo sie ein Querholz in (den) Boden pfahlen,
dort muß ich hin auf blutigen Sandalen
und bin der Sklave meiner alten Qualen,
mir wachsen Nägel aus den Wundenmalen,
und die Minuten pressen mich ans Kreuz.

opening wide, then shutting—bluish-thin;
quietly rose, and quietly sank in
his slight, hurt chest; the pale lips came apart
as if to form a word that, sick with aching,
now forced its way through rows of ivory:
"Why hast thou, oh my God, forsaken me?"
And as I heard him, by that dark word shaken,
that word whose meaning could not be mistaken,
and stood, and stood, and nothing else could see,—
then lightly from the Crucifixion Tree
he loosed his white hands, groaning: "I am he."
I listened long, until the echo fled;—
I saw the walls, decked by a garish drape;
my fingers touched this waxen toy, the shape
which smelled of lamp-oil. Breathlessly he said:
"This is my curse. Since my disciples, led
to folly by vainglorious boasts of faith,
plundered my body from the pit of death,
there's been no place where I could lay my head.
As long as stars will find their brightness pearled
in every brook, as long as sunlight calls
the spring to come back with its bacchanals,
so long must I keep wandering through the world.
From rood to rood I travel, penance-bound:
each time men drive a cross into the ground,
once more—in bloody shoes—I seek that mound;
the agony of old returns to hound
and humble me; a nail grows from each wound;
the minutes fasten me unto the rood.

67

So leb ich, ewig sterbend, meines Heuts
maßlose Reue. Krank und lang entkräftet,
da in der Kirche Kälte festgeheftet,
dort in dem Prunk profaner Jahrmarktsbuden;
ohnmächtig heut und doch gebetumschmachtet,
ohnmächtig morgen und dabei verachtet,
ohnmächtig ewig in der Sonnenhelle
des Kreuzwegs wie im Frieren der Kapelle.
So treib ich wie ein welkes Blatt umher.
Kennst du die Sage von dem Ewigen Juden?
Ich selbst bin jener alte Ahasver,
der täglich stirbt um täglich neu zu leben;
mein Sehnen ist ein nächtig-weites Meer,
ich kann ihm Marken nicht noch Morgen geben.
Das ist die Rache derer, die verdarben
an meinem Wort. Die opfernd für mich starben,
sie drängen hinter mir in weiten Reihn.
Horch! Ihre Schritte!—Horch! Ihr kreischend Schrein.

Doch eine große Rache nenn ich mein:
Ich weiß, bei jedem neuen Herbste warben
die Menschen um den Saft, den feuerfarben
die roten Reben ihrer Freude leihn.
Mein Blut fließt ewig aus den Nagelnarben,
und alle glauben es: mein Blut ist Wein,
und trinken Gift und Glut in sich hinein . . .

Thus, ever dying, endlessly renewed,
I live: each day another cross to bear;
impaled here in the chill of churches, there
in the profane booth of a gaudy fair;
strengthless today, yet plied by sickening prayer;
strengthless tomorrow, mocked at everywhere;
strengthless forever in the morning gold
of crossroads just as in the chapel's cold.
I drive, a dying leaf, the wide world through.
You know the myth of the Eternal Jew?
I am myself that Ahasueras old
who dies each day, that each day he may live;
a dark, wide sea's my yearning; I can give
no coin to comfort it, nor a tomorrow.
Thus they avenge themselves, who came to sorrow
through what I told them. Martyred for my sake,
an endless legion follows in my wake.
Listen! their tread!—the clamor that they make! . . .

But no less mighty a revenge is mine:
I know the grapes are crushed at harvest-time
so that the burning juice of the red vine
may bring to men the joy for which they pine.
My blood keeps flowing from the wounds forever,
and all, believing that my blood is wine,
pour down their throats my venom and my fever . . ."

68

Mich hielt das fürchterliche Prophezein
in bangem Bann. Aus hilfloser Hypnose
riß mich die Menge, die vorüberschwamm.
Ein Schwarm trat ein und fand sich mit Getose
bei jener ersten Gruppe just zusamm,
und vor mir hing der gelbe regungslose
Gekreuzigte in wächsner Jahrmarktspose
an seinem Stamm.

This dreadful prophesying held me long
in terror. Streaming past, the people tore me
out of a trance whose grip on me was strong.
A crowd came in and stood, with noisy tongue,
near that first group of figures, and before me
the body of the Crucified now hung
sallow and still; no more did he relax
the pose of wax.

69

DER NARR

Der Turm ruft in gewohnter Pose
den Mittag aus. Ins Sommerglühn
prallt schon die Kinderschar, die lose,
heraus vom Schulbankplattengrün:
So brechen wohl nach bangem Mühn
gefangne Falter freiheitskühn
aus dumpfer, grüner Forscherdose
und suchen eine rote Rose
und schwärmen werbend um ihr Blühn.—
Die Buben bilden kleine Truppen,
es wird gerauft, es wird marschiert,
wenn hurtig zu der Mutter Suppen
auch schon so mancher desertiert.
Die Mädel aber stehn wie Puppen
im Auslagfenster des Bazars
beisamm in bunten Plaudergruppen.
Und wagt ein Kleiner sie zu stuppen
am Zopfbandzipfel ihres Haars,
dann wenden sie sich: Welcher wars?
Und meistens flieht der junge Mars
vor ihrem Zürnen um die Ecke.
Und bei Geplauder und Genecke
verflattert mählich erst der Schwarm.—
Die kleine Anna, blond und arm,
packt jetzt als ob sie was entdecke
die nächste Freundin wie im Schrecke

THE LOON

The tower, as usual, peals out noon.
Set free, the troops of pupils soon
come bounding from their benches' green
into the radiance of June.
Such is the boldness to be seen
when captive wings at last unclose
their damp, green inquisition room
and roam until they find a rose
and, wooing, swarm about her bloom.
The boys are marshalled into troops:
they march about, they wage a war,
till, tempted by their mothers' soups,
deserters leave them by the score.
The girls, though, gossip on in groups
like brightly colored dolls that are
displayed in stores at a bazaar.
And if a lad is not afraid
to pull the ribbon of some braid,
they turn: Who did it? Like as not,
the youthful Mars will flee that spot
before a female cannonade.
And bantering, and chattering,
the swarms of revelers take wing.—
Now little Anna: poor, blonde thing,
seizes her playmate by the shoulder
with news that makes the blood run colder

70

und weist scheu flüsternd nach der Hecke
und ruft dann etwas. Wie Alarm
fährts in die Schar; der ganze Haufen
zerstiebt. Ein Stoßen und ein Laufen,
ein Wortgewirr, ein Stimmgeschnarr:
"Der Narr."

"Kinder!"
Und geschwinder
stürzt er herbei.
Ins Geschrei.
"Halt."
Seine hohe Gestalt
mit dem blassen Gesicht
ist immer dicht
hinter der Flucht.
Er sucht.
Mit den gekrallten
sehnenden Händen,
mit den kalten
Augen, die blenden,
will er sie halten,
will er sie wenden.
Flatternd in Falten
wallt um die Lenden
der Mantel. Die Lode
hemmt ihm die Flucht.
Bleich wie im Tode

and, shyly whispering, points out
the hedge, and then begins to shout.
The whole battalion's put to rout.
A scuffling, scuttering about,
words tangled, voices out of tune:
"The Loon!"

"Children!"
With bewildering
strides
he overtakes their cries.
"Stop!"
His great height,
his death-white cheeks,
follow their flight,
pursue their shrieks.
He seeks.
With yearning hands open
like talons groping—
with cold, unseeing
eyes—he is hoping
to keep them from fleeing,
to capture their eyes.
Around his thighs
the cloak is flapping,
its coarse wool trapping
him, as he flies.
Death in his cheeks,

steht er und sucht.
Und die Kinder entsetzt
und in Hitze gehetzt
hasten vorbei.
Auch Anna. Und jetzt,
er schaut sie—ein Schrei.
Er bricht durch die Reih
und faßt sie und fetzt
ihr das Kleidchen entzwei:
"Steh!"
Und dem armen Kind ist zum Sterben weh.
Rings schaut es nach Hilfe. Doch schreckenjäh
ist der Schwarm in den Gassen und Gärten zerstoben.
Und bebend hebt sie die Augen nach oben
bang und beklemmt.
Hat er ein Wunder getan?
Sie staunt ihn an:
die Augen des Fremden sind ihr nicht fremd.
Und es überkommt sie ein großes Vertraun.
Ihr ist: als wär sie lang krank gewesen,
hätt müssen zur dumpfigen Decke schaun
und dürfte des lachenden Blicks Genesen
zum Himmel nun heben, zum maitagblaun.
Sie fühlt: er läßt seine Rechte sinken
auf ihren Scheitel und kost ihn still,
und sie hascht wie im Traum nach der fiebernden
                                        Linken,

he stands and seeks.
And the children in dread
and with feverish brow
hasten ahead.
There's Anna. And now
he sees her—a wild
cry. Pushes through
and seizes the child;
her smock's torn in two:
"Stop!"
Half-dead with anguish, ready to drop,
she looks 'round for help. But none remain:
frightened, they vanish in garden and lane.
And quiveringly the girl looks up,
cringes and cowers.
Has he wrought a miraculous change?
She gapes again:
the eyes of the stranger cease to be strange.
And a great trust suddenly overpowers
her spirit: as if she had long been sick,
with musty bedding to stare at for hours,
till her eyes recovered their laughing trick
by drinking the blue of the Mayday air.
She feels: his right hand touches her hair
and gently, caressingly lingers there,
and as if in a dream she gropes for the left

weil sie sie küssen will . . .
Doch die Hand entflieht ihr hastig und heiß,
auf die langenden Händchen fällt eine Träne,
und die fremden Lippen fragen sie leis:
"Heißt deine Mutter nicht Magdalene?"
"Ja."
Und die fremden Lippen fragen so warm:
"Ist sie sehr arm?"
"Ja."
Und Lippen klingen wie Glockenerz:
"Hat sie viel Schmerz?"
"Ja.
Weil ich sie oft tief in der späten
Nacht noch sitzen und weinen sah."
"Kannst du auch beten?"
"Ja."
"Betest du denn auch für deinen Papa?"
"Ja."
"Tu's."
"Aber wo ist mein Papa . . . weißt du's?"
Und da hebt der Fremde das Kind empor.
Seine Stimme ist wie ein Vogelchor
der sich tief in erblühtem Jasmin verlor:
"Sag mir einmal das Wort noch vor!"
"Was?"
"Das."

to kiss it. But his hand
escapes with a motion fevered and swift;
on her hungering hand there falls a gift—
a tear—and the strange lips softly demand:
"Is Magdalene your mother's name?"
"Yes."
And the words on his lips are warm as flame:
"Is she in great distress?"
"Yes."
And the words on his lips ring out like chimes:
"Has she much sorrow?"
"Yes.
I have seen her sit up many times
crying from midnight until tomorrow."
"Do you know how to pray?"
"Yes."
"For your papa—have you prayers to say?"
"Yes."
"Do."
"But where's my papa? I don't know . . . Do you?"
At this he lifts her high as he can.
Like a choir of birds is the voice of the man,
birds lost deep in a blossoming glen
of jasmine: "Give me that word again!"
"What?"
"That."

73

"Papa?"
"Ja."
Und sein *Ja* ist ein jubelnder Siegessang.
Er küßt dem Kinde die Stirne lang,
er küßt dem Kinde die Augen blank;
sein Kuß ist Liebe, sein Kuß ist Dank.
Und er stellt das Kind wieder leis auf die Steine
und spricht: "Ich kann dir nichts geben, Kleine—"
Ein müdes Lächeln nur wirft er ihm zu:
"Ich bin ja viel ärmer als du. . . ."
Es war ein Weinen, wie er das sprach.
Und er winkt noch einmal leis mit der Hand
und geht. Er geht durch das heiße Land
wie ein Bettler im schlotternden Lodengewand
und doch wie ein König so stolz und groß.
Und sie haben ihn immer 'der Narr' genannt.
Und Anna steht lange, wie traumgebannt
staunt sie ihm nach,
dann stürmt sie nach Hause atemlos.—

Der Mutter Alles zu sagen, sie scheuts.
Doch plötzlich sagt sie beim Schlafengehn:
"Du, Mutter, ich hab einen Mann gesehn,
der war—wie der Mann am Kreuz. . . ."
. . . .

❖   ❖   ❖

74

"Papa?"
"Yes."
And that Yes is a victory-chant, a hurrah.
Long do his lips her forehead press;
he drinks her bright eyes with a kiss;
that kiss is love, is gratefulness.
And he sets her down tenderly, murmuring:
"I cannot give you anything—"
Only a smile: lips wearily curl:
"I am much poorer than you are, girl . . ."
Under the words there sounds a sob.
And lightly he motions once more with his hand,
and goes. He goes through the torrid land
like a beggar in his slovenly garb
and yet like a king, so proud and tall.
And he is named "Loon" by one and all.
Long in a trance does Anna gape
at the vanishing shape,
then homeward breathlessly storms away.

What has happened to her she does not say,
but at bedtime suddenly she speaks:
"Mother, I saw a man today—
like the man on the crucifix. . . ."
. . . .

❖   ❖   ❖

DIE NACHT

Nach Mitternacht ists. Dunkle Stunden gängeln
die Letzten heimwärts längs der Häuserreih.—
Nur im verrauchten Saale 'Zu den Engeln'
auf dem verschoßnen Samtsitz lehnen Zwei.
Er und ein Weib. Und gelbe Kellner bengeln
müd, mürrisch mahnend an dem Tisch vorbei.
Ein Piccolo hockt an des Saales Ende
auf steilem Stuhle ganz von Schlaf verschneit.
Nur da und dort glühn trübe Lampenbrände,
in Rauch und Dämmer lösen sich die Wände,
und langsam durch die Wanduhr tropft die Zeit.—
Das Weib neigt sich zu dem Gefährten. Weit
giert aus dem wellengrellen Seidenkleid
die Sinnenhast der ewig kalten Hände:
"Was bist du denn so traurig fort, du, Blasser?
Ich glaube gar du bist ein Menschenhasser?
Schau,—ich bin schön und wir sind ganz allein . . .
Die Schönheit! Prosit! Aber—du,—mit Wasser? . ."
Und sie erweckt ein Echo: "Kellner, Wein!"
"Nein, du, ich will nicht trinken," wehrt er ernst.
"Geh, Lieber, spare deine weisen Worte.
Willst du auch *jetzt* noch nicht? Schau her: die Sorte
Champagner! Schau! Ich wette daß du's lernst.
Bist du kein Freund von solchen Bacchanalen?
Schau dieses Perlenkämpfen, wie das schäumt,
schau dieses Perlendämpfen, wie sichs bäumt:

NIGHT

It's after twelve. Along the row of houses
dark hours coax home the last of the carousers.
But in the smoke-filled "Angel Room" a pair
still lean back in the frayed old velvet chair.
He and a woman. And a sallow waiter
reminds them rudely that it's getting later.
At the room's end there cowers a piccolo
upon a high stool, buried in the snow
of slumber. Just a few sad lampfires glow;
in smoke and dusk the walls begin to swim;
and Time drips gradually through the clock.—
The woman now is bending over him.
Out of the heaving of her silken frock
lust ever-icy hands: "What makes you mope,
you, pale one? Maybe you're a misanthrope?
I do believe you're somewhat in that line:
Look—I am pretty—and there's just us two . . .
To Beauty! Cheers! But—you—water for you? . . ."
And she awakes an echo: "Waiter, wine!"
Earnestly he resists: "No, I don't want to."
"Go on, don't waste your clever words, my dear.
You *still* don't want to? even now? See here:
champagne! Just wait! I wager you'll get onto
the knack of it. You'd rather not be won to
such bacchanal? See how this pearl-war dances;
this stew of pearls, see how it foams and prances:

Das ist der Weihrauch unsrer Kathedralen,
der prickelnd sickert aus opalnen Schalen!
Trink jetzt! Die Liebe lebe! . . Ausgeträumt!—"
Und sie schlürft tief das Schaumgold des Pokals
und läßt ihn, leer, im roten Schimmer blinken,
und löst dann leise mit der weißen Linken
die schweren Falten ihres Schultershawls.
Und wie wenn sacht des Meeres Wellen sinken
und aus der Flut im Glanz des Mainachtstrahls
die Inseln tauchen mit den Silberzinken,
so schimmert jetzt im Wogenqualm des Saals
ihr Marmorhals. Und ihre Hände winken
dem blassen Nachbar, suchend sehnsuchtleis.
"Komm!" lispelt sie "und willst du ewig säumen?"
Sie neigt sich näher und ihr Wort ist heiß:
"Noch bist du jung! Komm, sei kein Tor! ich weiß
was Beßres, als das Leben dumpf verträumen:
das Leben leben! Nimm dir deinen Preis."
Da packt es ihn, den neidlos, freudlos Kalten,
und ganz im Bann verhaltener Gewalten
wird alle Kraft in seiner Seele frei.
Er faßt das Weib mit einem wilden Schrei
und seine Finger krallt er in die Falten,
und gleißend reißt das Seidenkleid entzwei.

76

trickling from our cathedrals' opal bowls,
this is the incense—prickling prayerful souls!
Drink down! Long life to love! The vanished dreams!"
She takes a deep swig of the foaming gold,
in the red light her empty goblet gleams,
and with her white hand frees the shawl—it streams
down from her shoulder, fold by heavy fold.
And just as when the sea-wave gently sinks,
and from the flood, lit by a Maynight moon,
the isles emerge amid the silver-zincs,
so now in the smoke-billowing saloon
her throat of marble gleams. Her yearning hands
beckon the deathly one who never drinks.
"Will you forever dawdle?" she demands
lispingly; "Come!" and closer to him bends,
with hot words: "You're a young man yet; get wise!
Come, I know better than to dream away
a life: life should be lived! Now take your prize!"
The grudgeless, joyless cold one's in her sway;
his cravings, that so long were held at bay,
now burst their bonds within his soul, and rise!
He clasps the woman with a madman's cries;
his fingers clutch and claw the folds till they
ecstatically rip her silk array.

Die irren Hände wuchten schwer wie Blei,
als wollt er aus dem Leib sich neu gestalten
ein Götterbild, das seiner würdig sei.
Um ihre Glieder brandet Raserei.
So stürmt der Sturzbach, den das Eis gehalten,
aus seiner dumpfen Dämmerschlucht herbei
und springt und ringt und greift in alle Spalten
und seine Liebe tötet fast den Mai.
Mit wildem Griff zerrt er den Vorhang zu,
und in der Luft sind nur die süßen Klagen,
die wie ein Jubel klingen aus den Tagen,
da keiner noch in schämigem Getu
der Glieder Kraft in Fetzen eingeschlagen,
und jeder Wunsch war damals noch ein Wagen.—
Da fährt der blasse Mann aus schlaffer Ruh
und raunt dem müden Weibe glühend: "Du,"
er lauscht umher—, "ich muß dir etwas sagen.
Sie kamen einst mich bei Gericht verklagen.
Der Richter rief. Das war ein seltsam Fragen:
Ich hörs noch immer: *Bist du Gottes Sohn?*
Ich kann nicht mehr begreifen dieses Sinns,
doch damals ließ ich schelten mich und schlagen
und dachte, aufgehetzt durch ihren Hohn,
es muß mein Stolz bis an die Sterne ragen.
Ich schrie sie an: *Was wollt ihr? Ja, ich bins.*
Zu meines Vaters Rechten ist mein Thron!

Heavy as lead, his hands now go astray
as if he wishes from that form of clay
to mold a shape divine enough for him.
Delirium breaks 'round her, limb by limb.
Just so the cataract, which ice has bound,
bursts from its gully with a savage sound,
to seize all clefts, to plunge and lunge around,
till in its ardor May is almost drowned.
Wildly he draws the curtain; and the air
holds nothing but the sweet laments, that chime
like jubilation echoed from a time
before the human race, grown modest, chose
to bind the power of its limbs in clothes,
and every wish was yet a thing to dare.—
The pale man wakens from his slack repose
and, making certain no one else is there,
he whispers: "You, there's something I must say.
They came to arraign me in the court one day.
The judge cried out. His question was so odd:
I hear it still: *Are you the son of God?*
No longer am I sure of what it meant,
but at the time I let them lash and chide;
and, stirred up by their scorn, I thought my pride
would reach the top star in the firmament.
What do you want? Yes, I am he, I cried.
My throne is stationed at my sire's right side.

77

Was lachst du, Weib? So spei mir ins Gesicht.
ich weiß es, ich verdiene deinen Spott.
Und meine Reue. Nein, ich bin es nicht,
ich bin kein Gott! . . ."
                    "Du kannst nicht viel vertragen,
mein Lieber. Welch ein drolliges Gegirr.
Kaum wirbelt noch ein Glas dir aus dem Magen
zu Herz und Hirn, schon sprichst du wahn und wirr.—
Nein, nein, du bist nicht Gott, mach dir nicht Sorgen,
und niemand wird dich so verklagen. Nein.
Doch wart du Blasser, bis zum nächsten Morgen
sollst du ein wenig König sein.
Ja, willst du? Wart, ich werde wenn mirs glückt
aus diesen Rosen dir die Krone schmieden.
Und sind sie nicht mehr frisch, gieb dich zufrieden,
mein hoher Herr, du hast sie selbst zerdrückt . ."—
Und ihre Finger fügen jetzt geschickt
zu krausem Kranze Rose an um Rose,
auch welke Blätter sind hineingestickt.
Sie legt ihn auf das Haupt, das regungslose
aus leeren Augen ihr entgegenblickt,
dann klatscht sie in die Hände, lacht und nickt:
"Bravissimo, die echte Königspose!"

—Why are you laughing? So, spit in my face;
I know it, woman; I deserve your sneer
and my remorse. No, I am not—that's clear—
I'm not a god! . . ."
                    "You can't take much, I fear.
Such funny talk! Before one glass can race
out of your stomach to the heart and brain,
your words become unreal and half-insane.—
No, no, you are not God, that's very plain;
nor shall you be accused of such a thing.
But wait, you pale one! till tomorrow's sun,
you shall be somewhat of a king.
That suits you? Wait, if I can get it done,
I'll turn these flowers into your coronet.
And if they've lost their freshness, don't forget:
you yourself crushed them, my exalted one! . . ."—
and dexterously now her fingers braid
rose unto rose until the wreath is made,
including leaves that have begun to fade.
She sets it on his head which, never moving,
looks empty-eyed upon her all the while;
then, laughing, she applauds, her nod approving:
"Bravissimo, the true imperial style!"

Schon kommt der Morgen nach den Scheiben zielen;
die ersten Speere stecken in den Dielen
hell, wie sie just durchs fahle Fenster fielen.
Und gegenüber schmiltzt schon auf dem Dach
die Dämmerung. Da gähnt das Weib sich wach
und steckt das Kleid sich auf, das Gierde jach
ihr von der Schulter riß. Dann denkt sie nach
und friert und gähnt: "Willst du noch König spielen?"
Sie zerrt ihn auf und murmelt: "Toller Tropf,
willst du mit deiner Krone auf dem Kopf
bei Tage heut nach Haus spazieren gehn?"
Er starrt sie an und kann sie nicht verstehn.
Da streift sie ihm mit mürrischem Gebaren
den dürren Herbstkranz aus den schwarzen Haaren.
Er starrt sie an—und weint, wie von der Stirne
die letzte morgenwelke Rose fällt:
"Wir sind der ewge Erbfluch dieser Welt:
Der ewige Wahn ich—du die ewige Dirne."

But Dawn takes aim against the panes, and leaves
his first shafts in the boards: bright shafts that fall
through the pale window, and are fixed in the wall.
And dusk is melting from the nearby eaves.
She yawns herself awake, and gets the gown
back on, that passion brusquely had pulled down.
Then she recalls, and yawns—her cold limbs aching:
"Still ready to play king, are you?" and shaking
the man awake, she murmurs: "Crazy clown,
you wouldn't mind, right now in daylight, taking
a promenade outdoors, decked in your crown?"
He stares, uncomprehending. With a frown
she brushes the dead autumn wreath he wore
from his black hair. He stares at her once more,
and weeps, as the last withered leaves disperse
and the last faded rose falls to the floor:
"We are this world's eternal inbred curse:
I, the eternal loon—you, the eternal whore."—

79

VENEDIG

Die junge Nacht liegt wie ein kühler Duft
auf dem Canal, und grauer nun und greiser
sind die Paläste und die Gondeln leiser,
als führte jede einen toten Kaiser
in seine Gruft.
Und viele fahren, aber eine schwenkt
jetzt scheu und ängstlich in die tiefsten Gassen,
weil tiefste Liebe oder tiefstes Hassen
ihr Steuer lenkt.
Vor einem Marmorhaus mit staubger Zier
drängt sie sich horchend an die Wappenpfähle.
Und lange ruhte keine Gondel hier.
Die Stufen warten.—Fern aus heller Kehle
am Canal grande singt ein Gondolier,
und suchend irrt sein Lied durch die Kanäle.
Der Fremde steht und trinkt den Klang voll Gier,
in lauter Lauschen löst sich seine Seele:
Vorrei morir . . . .

Der Abend zog vorbei am Erdgeschoß
des Dogenhofs, und die Reflexe rannten
hin wie ein Schwarm von wunden Flagellanten.
Er aber stand so einsam ernst und groß
am Fuß der stolzen Treppe der Giganten,
und seiner Blicke dunkle Bogen spannten
sich nach dem Fenster, dessen Flächen brannten:

VENICE

The young night, like a fresh aroma, lies
on the canal; the palaces become
older and grayer; and the gondolas' hum
grows soft, as though in each a dead king nighs
his dark new realm.
And many sail, but one of them now veers
into the deepest streets, for at its helm
either the deepest love or deepest hate
stands and steers.
Before a mansion, dustily ornate,
it hearkens at the blazoned columns. Here
no gondola delays. The great steps wait—
out on the Grand Canal, a gondolier
pours forth a melody from his pure throat,
and searchingly his song strays far and near
through the canals. The stranger drinks each note;
he listens, till his soul is set afloat:
Vorrei morir. . . .

Here once the doge held court: now evening came
past the ground floor, and its reflections ran
like flagellants self-scourged and cleansed of blame.
Alone, though, tall and serious, the man
stood where those titans' haughty stairs began;
and the dark arches of his gaze did span
toward one window-glass that seemed aflame:

sie heißen es das Fenster Pellico's.
Er nickte leise, so als stände jener
noch dort, der einst in ewig öder Haft
ergeben wie ein echter Nazarener
verzichtete auf Zorn und Kampf und Kraft.
Vielleicht giebt er den Gruß zurück und rafft
des Vorhangs Falten. Wenn noch seinen Namen
Verliebte, (die) des Wegs vorüberkamen,
zusammenträumen mit den Sündendramen,
erschien er hoch im heißen Fensterrahmen,
er lächelte das Lächeln einer zahmen
in Fesseln müd gewordnen Leidenschaft.—
Und jener unten lächelte es mit.
Dann stieg er stufenan mit scheuem Schritt
und stand oft still, im vollen Abendscheine,
drin die Arkaden, wie versteinte Haine,
zu harren schienen, daß er sie durchweine,
so traurig war er; denn es war der Eine,
der immer dankte, wenn er sprach: ich litt.
Sein Haupt war schwer, und schweren Fußes ging
er in die leeren Marmorbogengänge,
an denen wie vergessenes Gepränge
der rote, raschverwelkte Abend hing.
Ihn fröstelte, und hastig ward sein Schreiten,
das bang erklang im hallend langen Gang.
Vor seiner eignen Lehre war ihm bang:
vor jener Lehre der Vergänglichkeiten.
Sie wuchs um ihn in säulenstarrem Hohne:

"Pellico's window" is its common name.
He nodded quietly, as if tonight
that prisoner of old could still be seen
submissive as a genuine Nazarene
despising wrath and violence and might.
Perhaps he'd see him nod, and do the same,
and pull aside the curtain-folds. When they
who loved his name, came from across the way
under the spell of a morality play,
he used to stand there in the window-frame,
he used to smile the smile of a great passion
which manacles had left fatigued and tame.—
And he, below, smiled back in the same fashion.
Then timidly he climbed, and often stood
stock-still in moonlight magically flashing
where each arcade, changed to a petrified wood,
seemed hopeful he would rend it with a moan,
so mournful was he: for he was the One
who always sounded grateful when he said
"I suffered." Bowed of head, with heavy tread,
he took the arches' marble paths alone
on which the red, swift-withered evening shone
like ornaments whose meaning once was known.
He shivered, and in haste he strode ahead,
echoing weirdly down the corridor.
He had become afraid of his own lore:
that what is now is soon to be no more.
'Round him like pillared scorn this creed had grown:

81

so wächst der Zorn dem rachegieren Sohne,
der aus des greisen Vaters feiger Frohne
zu eignem Wort und eignem Weh sich wand.
Er lief zuletzt. Und wie gerettet stand
er endlich still auf einsamem Balkone
und lauschte, was in langem, leisem Tone
die matte Woge sang dem Abendland.

Da knistert neben ihm ein Schleppgewand:
und bei ihm kniet in hoher Mützenkrone
mit weißem Bart ein purpurner Padrone,
und leise faltet sich die Hand zur Hand.
Und Jesus nickt und fragt den alten Mann:
"Schwarz ist der Hafen. Wo sind eure Feste?
Giebts keine Gäste mehr? An die Paläste
legt niemals mehr der bunte Jubel an?
Ich warte schon so lange, wo sind sie
die mich verehrt, die wundersamen Alten
mit Silberbärten, lang und tiefgespalten—
die Vendramin und Papadopoli.
Ich weiß: die Nacht bewohnt in euren kalten
Palästen jetzt das beste Prunkgemach.
Denn ihr seid lang gestorben, und den Jungen
ist Lied und Lachen gar so bald verklungen
in einer Zeit, die nur mit Eisen sprach.
Jetzt sind die Gassen alle kalt und brach,

so the son's vengeful wrath grows high and higher
who, from the craven whim of his gray sire,
turned to a word, a sorrow all his own.
At last he ran. And like a ransomed soul,
upon a balcony he came to rest,
and listened to the long, low barcarole
the languid wave was singing to the West.

Nearby him sounds the crackling of a gown:
and in an elevated bonnet-crown
there kneels a doge: white-bearded, purple-dressed,
one hand of his within the other pressed.
And Jesus asks the old man, nodding slightly:
"The harbor's black. Have you no revels nightly?
the guests all gone? the laughter dispossessed
from palaces which used to frolic brightly?
I have been waiting for so many years!
Where are the grand old men who worshipped me,
the ones with long and deep-cleft silver beards,
the Vendramin and Papadopoli?
I know: in your cold palaces' most choice
apartments, night is nesting in the rafter.
For you are long since dead, and song and laughter
died soon enough for those who followed after—
died in an age that spoke with iron voice.
The streets are cold now, scarce a rudder ploughs,

und Trauer nur, in halbem Traum gesungen,
langt oft den flüchtenden Erinnerungen
aus einem engen grauen Hause nach.
Von keinem Landen wissen eure Stufen,
und alles kam, wie es die Vorsicht will.
Der Hochmut hohe Häuser starben still,
und nur die Kirchen dauern noch und rufen."

   "Ja, Herr," spricht jetzt der Doge und entfaltet
die Hände nicht. "Des Todes Ohnmacht waltet
mit tausend tiefen Schauern über uns.
Und deine Glocken locken lauten Munds.
Du giebst noch immer große, reiche Feste
und machst, daß deine gernbereiten Gäste
in deinen Hallen Elend und Gebreste
vergessen und wie Kinder selig sind.
Und jedes Volk, das gerne noch als Kind
sich fühlen mag, folgt in die Prachtpaläste
die du ihm aufgetan und betet blind.
Doch ich bin alt. Ich seh die Zeiten rollen
bis in den Tag, da keine Völker mehr
wie Kinder sein und Kinder spielen wollen;
denn mögen alle deine Glocken grollen,
dann bleibt auch dein Palast für ewig leer."
Der Alte schwieg. Wie betend blieb er knien.
Sternknospen sprangen an den Himmelsachsen.
Und dieses Knien schien weit hinauszuwachsen
vorbei an Christo und weit über ihn . . .

❖ ❖ ❖

and only sorrow, sung in a half-dream,
keeps reaching for remembrances that seem
to be escaping from a strait, gray house.
Your steps don't know of other lands; and all
has come as if by providence. In pride
the highest houses quietly have died,
and only churches still endure and call."

   "Yes, lord," the doge replies, without unfolding
his hands. "The feebleness of death is holding
us subject, with a thousand shuddering-spells.
And with reverberating mouths your bells
allure us. Still you hold great festivals,
and to the eager guests within your halls
you offer a communion that dispels
all misery, and makes them grow as gay
as children. And desiring nothing else
than childhood, people throng the citadels
you've opened up to them, and blindly pray.
But I am old. I see the seasons turning
until the day when nations will no more
for childhood's way and childhood play be yearning;
then, even though your bells keep up their churning,
the dust will gather on your palace-floor."
The old one hushed: prayerlike, upon his knee.
Starbuds broke out on heaven's axle-tree.
This kneeling seemed to blossom forth, to rise
past Christ, and far beyond him toward the skies.

❖ ❖ ❖

DIE KINDER

Das war
ein Mann inmitten einer Kinderschar.
Schlicht um die Schultern lag ihm der Talar,
und heimathell war ihm das Heilandshaar.
Und wie um einen frühen Frühlingstag
sich, jäherwacht, die Blüten staunend scharen,
so kamen Kinder zu dem Wunderbaren,
den keiner von den Alten nennen mag.
Die Kinder aber kennen ihn schon lang
und drängen in das offne Tor der Arme—
ein blasses betet: Du bist das 'Erbarme,'
nach dem die Mutter ihre Hände rang.
Und leise flüstert ihm das wangenwarme:
"Nichtwahr, du wohnst im Sonnenuntergang,
dort wo die Berge groß und golden sind.
Dir winkt der Wipfel und dir singt der Wind,
und guten Kindern kommst du in die Träume."
Da neigen alle sich wie Birkenbäume.
Es neigen sich die Blonden und die Braunen
vor seinem Lächeln, und die Alten staunen.
Und Kinder flüchten sich von allen Seiten
in seinen Segen heim wie in ein Haus,
und lauschen alle. Seine Worte breiten
weit über sie die weißen Flügel aus:

THE CHILDREN

There stood
amid the children of the neighborhood
a man. His garment was of modest wear,
and bright as home was his redeemer's-hair.
And just as on a day in early spring
the blossoms, suddenly awakened, stare,
so had the children gathered, marveling
at him, whom none of the adults would dare
to name. But he is well-known to the young,
who crowd the gateway of the city's poor.
One of the swarm—a pale one—murmurs: "You're
the Mercy for whose sake my mother wrung
her hands." The words are tender on her tongue:
"Your home is in the sunset—am I right? . . .
there, where the mountain-peaks are proud and bright.
To you the tree-tops nod; to you are sung
the windsongs; and you visit—like a friend—
good children in their dreams." At this they bend
like birches, all of them—the dark, the blonde—
before his smile—and the adults are stunned.
Unto his blessing, as if home were there,
come children scurrying from everywhere,
and all are listening. The word he brings
spreads over them the whiteness of its wings:

"Hat einmal eins von euch schon nachgedacht,
wie eilig euch die leisen Stunden führen
an jedem Tage und in jeder Nacht
durch tausend Tore und durch tausend Türen.
Noch gehn die Angeln alle leicht und leise
und alle Pforten fallen scheu ins Schloß;
noch bin ich Warner euch und Weggenoß,
doch weit aus meinen Reichen reift die Reise.
Ihr wollt ins Leben, und das bin ich nicht,
ihr müßt ins Dunkel, und ich bin das Licht,
ihr hofft die Freude, ich bin der Verzicht,
ihr sehnt das Glück und—ich bin das Gericht."
Er schwieg. Von ferne horchten auch die Großen.
Dann seufzte er: "Ihr müßt mich nicht verstoßen,
wenn wir zusammen an den Marken stehn.
Mich mitzunehmen seid ihr dann zu jung;
doch schaut ihr mal zurück von euren Fahrten
vielleicht in einen armen Blumengarten,
vielleicht ins Mutterlächeln einer zarten
versehnten Frau, vielleicht in ein Erwarten:
Ich bin die Kindheit, die Erinnerung.
Gebt mir die Hand, schenkt mir (im) Weitergehn
noch einen Blick, der schon ins Leben tauchte,
aus dem der neue und noch niegebrauchte
Gott seine Hände euch entgegenhält.
Ihr dürft hinaus. Es wartet eine Welt."

"Is there among you one who meditates
how hastily the soundless hours lead you,
how day by day and night by night they speed you
through thousand doorways and through thousand   [gates?
And all the hinges move just as they need to,
and all the doors fall softly into place;
your conscience and your comrade I remain,
although the journey ripens past my reign.
I am not life, and life is what you're after;
the darkness is your portion—I illume;
'Renounce!' I cry—but you are lured by laughter;
you crave good fortune, and—my voice is doom."
He ceased. The grownups listened from afar.
Then, sighing, he continued. "When we are
balked at the border, don't abandon me.
You'll be too young to take me where you go;
but as you travel, turn back once to see:
perhaps in a poor place where flowers grow,
or in the tender smile of her who's been
a long time yearning, or perhaps within
an expectation: I am Memory,
and Childhood. Go—but as you seek strange lands,
turn back to offer me one final glance
already dipped in life from which the new
and never-prayed-to God holds out his hands.
Go on, then. There's a world awaiting you."

85

Sie horchten hastig seinem Verheißen,
ihre Wangen waren so warm:
"Werden wir an den Türen reißen?!"
ruft ein wilder Kleiner im Schwarm.
Und da bettelt er bang: "Du, führe
schnell uns weiter durch Wasser und Wald,
und die große, die letzte Türe
kommt sie dann bald?"

So an dem Glück, das der Meister verkündet,
haben sich hell seine Augen entzündet,
und er blüht in der Sonne auf.
Aber da hebt sich aus horchendem Hauf
einsam ein Kleiner, ihm weht das verworrne
welkende Harr um die Stirne gebläht
wie die zerrissene Zier überm Zorne
eines Helmes weht.
Seine Stimme flattert und fleht:
"Du!" er klammert um seine Knie
bange die armen hungernden Hände—
"Solche Worte vom ewigen Ende
sagtest du nie!
Wenn die anderen undankbaren
weiter wollen zu jagenden Jahren—
ich bin anders, anders wie sie!"
Und er umklammert im Krampfe die Knie.—

They hear, in haste, the promise he speaks;
warmer and warmer grow their cheeks:
"Shall we be pounding at the doors?!"
cries out a wild one in the throng—
cries out and anxiously implores:
"Through forest and flood, come speed us along!
And is the greatest door, the last,
soon to be passed?"

Thus, for the future the Master has vowed,
the eyes of that youngster boldly ignite;
and he blooms in the midday light.
But one, of that hushed and hearkening crowd,
lifts himself now, one child alone;
dishevelled and wilted his hair, wind-blown,
as over a helmet's rage still flies
proudly the torn prize.
The voice of this one flutters and begs:
"You!" He anxiously clasps his legs
with poor, starved hands: "You never
warned us, you never said
it would end forever!
Let the ungrateful gallop ahead
to years that the swiftest cannot recover—
I am different, different from these!"
And in a convulsion he clasps his knees.—

Und die Lippen des Lichten erbeben,
und er neigt sich dem Weinenden leise:
"Giebt die Mutter dir Spiel und Speise?"
Da schluchzt ihm der Knab in den Schooß:
"Zum Spielen bin ich zu groß."
"Bringt sie dir morgens ins Stübchen
deine Brühe warm?"
Da bebt das bangende Bübchen:
"Bin zum Essen zu arm."
"Küßt sie dir nie die Wange
mit ihrer Liebe rot?"
Da gesteht er: "Lange, lange
ist mir Mutter tot." . . .
Und die Lippen des Lichten erbeben
wie Blätter im herbstlichen Hain:
"Oh dann *warst* du schon draußen im Leben,
und wir können beisammen sein."

The lips of the radiant one, they quiver,
and he bends toward the weeping lad:
"Does mother give you games and food?"
Then into his lap sobs the boy:
"I'm too old for a toy."
"Does she bring you broth, fresh-brewed,
mornings when you wake?"
The lad has begun to quake:
"Too poor; I go unfed."
"Don't her kisses make
your cheeks sometimes turn red?"
Then he confesses: "Mother
has been a long time dead." . . .
And the bright one's lips are unsteady
as leaves in autumn weather:
"Then you've *been* out in life already,
and now we can stay here together."

87

DER MALER

Die alte Standuhr, von dem Zwölfuhrschlagen
noch immer müde, rief das 'Eins' so weh,
daß er zusammenzuckte und den Kragen
schnell um der Kleinen Schultern schmiegte: "Geh!"
Sie sah erstaunt ihn an beim Abschiedsagen
und bangte immer wieder mit der zagen
versagten Stimme, kinderklug: "Wann seh
ich dich denn wieder?" "Nun—in diesen Tagen,
geh, du bist lästig mit dem vielen Fragen."
Sie rief und fror und draußen fiel der Schnee.—

Er aber trat zurück ins Atelier
und ging mit stillen Schritten in dem kühlern
vertrauten Raume her und hin.
Das leise Licht, das wie mit feinen Fühlern
ins stumme Dunkel suchte vom Kamin,
erweckte da und dort ein Ding zum Leben,
das seltsam fremd in heimlichem Erheben
sich formte in der kurzen Gunst des Lichts.
In weichem Wechseln wogte Sein und Nichts
rings um den Mann, der sinnenden Gesichts
sich ganz verlor im scheuen Schattentreiben,
bis er, wie hart vor einem Hindernis,
den Fenstervorhang von den Riesenscheiben

THE PAINTER

The ancient time-piece, that had not yet found
its breath, after the toll of twelve, cried "One"
so feebly that he winced, in haste around
her shoulders wrapped the cape, and bid her: "Run!"
The girl observed him, as she said farewell,
with eyes agape; and once again her slow,
hesitant words with childish wisdom fell:
"When shall I see you?" "One of these days, Now go;
your questions bother me." She turned to yell
something, and froze, and outside fell the snow.

But he went back into the studio
and noiselessly began to pace
his homey, freezing quarters, to and fro.
The gentle light, which from the fireplace
groped in the silent gloominess as though
by means of feelers, here and there was giving
to some dead thing the miracle of living,
tricked into being by the light's brief grace.
Unreal—Real—that fluctuating twain,
wavered about the man of thoughtful face
who lost himself quite, in a shadow-play
until, as if some barrier blocked his way,
he ripped the curtain from the window-pane

fortzerrte, daß die Seide zischend riß.
Und da im Mond—die Dinge durften bleiben—
da blieb auch *der*, den er im Schatten schon
mit allen Sinnen seines Seins erkannte,
obwohl er nicht das Antlitz zu ihm wandte
und reglos auf die große weitgespannte
Bildleinwand schaute, drauf mit mattem Ton
der Silbermond die Winterlichter streute.
Sie sanken mitten in die Männermeute,
die einen Mann umdrängte und umdräute,
der blaß und ärmer wie die andern war.
Er stand wie ein Verräter in der Schar,
stand wie ein Leugner, den die Liebe reute,
und ohne alle Hoheit war sein Haar.
Und seine Würde war wie ein Talar
von seiner Brust gesunken, und es scheute
ein Kinderschwarm sich vor dem Proletar . .

Auf diesem Bilde jetzt die fremde Lichte
schien ein Geschenk zu sein von dem Gesichte
des Mannes, den der Maler davor fand;
in kalte Kanten krallte er die Hand,
und hingehetzt von hundert Ängsten floh
die Seele ihm mit feigem Flügelbreiten
zu allen Hoffnungen und Heimlichkeiten
und wähnt: sie wird bei *einer* die bereiten

so that the silk hissed at the gash he made.
Since, in the moonlight, all else may remain—
he (whom the painter sensed there, in the shade,
with all his consciousness) *he* also stayed;
he knew him, though he did not turn his head
but on a great wide canvas trained his sight:
a painting over which the moon had shed
a subtle tint of silver wintry light.
It fell amidst a mob that clawed and pressed
a captive man, whose face was far more white,
whose aspect was far poorer than the rest.
He stood there like a traitor in the rout,
a Nay-sayer, who rued his love, no doubt;
no hint of grandeur did his hair suggest.
And, like a gown, the honor of that man
sank from his breast, and swarms of children ran
in terror from the proletarian . . .

The eerie glow upon this canvas now
seems like a gift from that man's face, somehow—
that man the painter has discovered there;
the frame's cold corners now his fingers seize—
and, hounded by a hundred kinds of care,
his soul escapes upon her cowardly wing,
and seeks among all hopes and mysteries,
and dreams that she may find, in *one* of these,

89

Fritz von Uhde's *Christi Himmelfahrt,*
The Ascension of Christ, sketch, 1897.

Fritz von Uhde's *Christi Himmelfahrt,*
The Ascension of Christ, painting, 1897.

Fluchtfenster finden in das Nirgendwo.
Doch eh sie noch zurückgefunden,—gleiten
des Bleichen Blicke von dem Bild und leiten
das leise Wort: "Warum malst du mich so?"
"Bin ich denn so an deinem Bett gesessen,
wenn deine Furcht aus Kinderfiebern schrie,
und in dem Mahnen der Marienmessen—
war das die Miene, die dir Mut verlieh?
Und dann—am Grabe deiner Mutter—wie
entstieg ich da den zitternden Zypressen?
Hast du im Weiterschreiten mich vergessen,
und meine Züge, warum malst du sie?"
Sein Fragen senkte sich so frühlingsstill,
wie eine frühe Blüte sinkt vom Baume
die heil in Halmen harrt, ob tief im Traume
ein lieber Wind sie spielend wählen will,—
allein der Maler, scheu von Scham und Schuld,
zertritt die zarte mit der Ungeduld
des bangen Sklaven. Und sein Haß hält roh
die Faust ihm hin: "Ich sah dich immer so."
Und da wächst der, der wie ein Büßer stand,
weit auf. Sein Schatten hüllt die ganze Wand,
und seine Stimme schwillt wie eine Flamme:

92

flight-windows onto Nowhere opening.
But ere she flounders home,—the pale one's stare
turns from the painting, and accompanies
his gentle word: "Why do you paint me thus?
Did I sit thus beside your boyhood bed
when fever made you bellow forth your dread?
And in the Virgin's mass, admonishéd,
was this the mien that made you valorous?
And at your mother's grave—was this the way
I soared beyond the cypress-tops one day?
Have you forgotten me in all the rush
of striding on? And why do you portray
my face?" The question sinks with such a hush
as does an early blossom from a bush
who, on the blades unwounded, hopes she may
in dreams be chosen by a wind at play,—
but now the painter, irked by guilt and shame,
tramples the frail thing with a frightened slave's
impatience. And the fist his hatred waves
is raw: "To me you always looked the same."
And he, who seemed a penitent, grows tall.
His shadow covers the entire wall,
and suddenly his voice leaps forth like flame:

"So schien ich dir aus diesem Bettlerstamme?
Die zage, blasse Armut war mir Amme,
und drum glaubst *du*: es ist die Schergenschramme
auf meiner Brust mein einzig Purpurrecht?
Ich trank mir nicht den Adel aus dem Schwamme,
als König kürte ich mir ein Geschlecht,
und erst im Sterben ward ich Knecht.
Da ward ich—Gott. Und nur der niegewußte
Gott könnte groß sein, der nicht folgen mußte
dem ungestümen Ruf der Menge, die
ihn brünstig brauchte. Doch in wahngeblähter
Beharrlichkeit langt früher oder später
der Pöbel alle Götter aus dem Äther,
und in den bangen Blicken ihrer Beter
zerschmelzen sie."

Es schwand in Schwaden sein weißes Kleid,
es ging keine Pforte.
Aber der Maler hörte noch Worte,—
milde Worte wehten von weit
nicht aus der Zeit:
". . . In gleichem Harm und in gleichen Hemden
will ich frierend mit Freunden gehn,
aber vor den Seelenfremden
will ich festlich und fürstlich stehn:

"So, of this pauper-stock you thought I came?
You thought—because my pale, meek nursing-dame
was poverty—the soldier's mark, that small
scar on the breast, was my sole purple claim?
Not from the sponge I drank my noble pride;
the lineage was royal that I chose;
I was no slave, until I died.
Then I became—a god. And only those
among the gods are great, whom no one knows;
they need not answer the impetuous-throated
who crave a god, and frantically call.
But soon or late, the rabble, madness-bloated,
summons the gods from their celestial hall,
and in the desperate stare of the devoted
they melt, they fall."

In swaths his garment of white grows dim;
gateless he goes.
But the painter listens: words come to him,
kindly words from a distant clime,
not bound by Time:
". . . In matching grief and in matching clothes
freezing with my friends I'll range,
but before those to whose souls I am strange
into my princeliest garb I'll change:

93

Mal mich im Purpur dieses Blutes,
das wund von Wehen und Wundern war,
und mit der Mitra meines Mutes
hülle mir mein armes Haar.
Und alles Leuchten der Liebe—legs
an den Rand meiner Hände,
daß ich den Himmel ganz verschwende
an alle Kinder—unterwegs. . . ."

94

❖ ❖ ❖

paint me in purple: as this that flows,
this blood, galled forth by wonders and woes;
and with my mitre of gallantry
hide my poor hair, that none may see.
Bring all the lights of love to lie
in my fingers' care,
that as I pass I may squander the sky
upon all children . . . everywhere . . ."

❖ ❖ ❖

DIE KIRCHE VON NAGO

Diese Dörfer sind arm und klein;
du kommst nirgends hinaus und hinein,
nur ein paar Hütten, die dir begegnen
mitten im Mai.
Willst du sie segnen?
Sie sind schon vorbei.
Aber vor dir die Kirche steht
ragend im Abend höher oben
als hätte die Erde selber gehoben
aus kleinen Hütten ein großes Gebet.
Aber es muß schon lange sein
seit dies geschah:
vom Kreuzturm stürzte die Stange ein,
die Glocke schlief überm Klange ein—
niemand war da.
Haben im Dorf wohl das Beten vergessen—
oder beten sie anderswo?
Sie denken: ohne die teuern Messen
geht das Sterben auch so.
Und lassen es über die Reben regnen
und lassen es über die Rosen scheinen
und vergessen das Lachen und kennen kein Weinen
und sind doch die Deinen:
Willst du sie segnen?

THE CHURCH OF NAGO

These villages are poor and small;
no exits or entrances at all;
just a few cottages that accost you
amid the May.
Would you bless them? Past you
they fall and away.
But before you the church-spire juts
high up into the evening air
as though earth herself had lifted a prayer,
a mighty prayer out of little huts.
This happened, though, in a bygone time:
lacking for care,
the steeple sank into ruin and grime;
the bell was lulled asleep by its chime—
no one was there.
Are the villagers blind to the doors that beckon—
or do they pray in some other place?
Who needs an expensive mass? they reckon;
death comes in any case.
And so they let it rain on the vine
and on the roses they let it shine
and forget how to laugh and know not of weeping
and are yet in your keeping:
have they your grace?

95

Du willst erst in deiner Kirche ruhn
und dann zurück zu den seltsam Frommen
hell von dämmernden Hängen kommen
und Wunder tun.
Weißt du schon, wie du dann ihr Weh
wirst bedenken?
Wirst du die Jungen aus den Gesenken
noch vor Tag auf den Hügel lenken
und von dort ihrem Schauen schenken
den Gardasee?
Wirst du die Berge, gleich Riesenpfühlen
näher rücken um dieses Tal,
daß die Alten mit einem Mal
sich heimlicher fühlen?
Denn du hast Mächte und Möglichkeiten
und die Dinge, die du rufst
werden dich wie einen König begleiten
und dir willige Brücken breiten
über die Meere, die du schufst.—
Aber heute bist du schon matt. Und dein Kleid
ist bestaubt.
Staubig dein Haupt.
Kommst du von weit?

96

First you wish to rest at your shrine;
then back to those who are truly religious
you shall come, bright, from the dusking ridges
with deeds divine.
And how to handle their grief, have you
been thinking?
Shall you lead from the vale young souls that are
onto the hills ere the sun wakes blinking,   [sinking,
and send their gaze from the summit, drinking
Lake Garda's blue?
Shall you push the peaks, like giants' pillows,
closer 'round this valley, to cheer
the spirits of the gray-haired fellows
with a cozier atmosphere?
For you've powers and possibilities,
and the things which stir at your summons
shall accompany you in your goings and comings
and build eager bridges over the seas
that came into being by your decrees.—
But today how faint you are!
Dusty now
your dress, your brow.
Have you come far?

Er sagt: "Mein Weg ist von Meer zu Meer.
Ich bin her
aus dem fernen Gestern
gekommen.
Und weiß nicht wie.
Meine Leiden, die weißen Schwestern
haben mich in die Mitte genommen . . .
Jetzt weinen sie."
Er schwieg.
Und ich hörte sie wirklich weinen
und sah, wie er zwischen steilen Steinen
langsam zu seiner Kirche stieg.
So war kein Sieg.
Das war die Heimkehr eines Ermatteten,
der viel geirrt,
und niemehr Hirt
und dunkel aller Beschatteten
Bruder wird.
Aber noch steht ihm das Haus
in welches ihr Beten
lange alle die Armen gebracht;
und wenn er es findet, wird es ihm Macht,
und er wird wie im Traum in fürstlicher Tracht
erwacht
nach raschem Ruhn
heraus
aus Trümmern treten
und Wunder tun.

"From sea to sea my pathway lies,"
he replies.
"I have come to thee
from distant years.
And don't know how.
My woes, the white sisters, have taken me
tenderly into their midst . . . Their tears
are falling now."
He ended.
And I heard them really moan
and saw how, slowly, from stone to stone
up toward his prayer-house he ascended.
No triumph splendid.
This was his homecoming, weary and sore,
who oft had strayed,
and would nevermore
herd sheep, and brotherhood darkly swore
to those in the shade.
But here it is, the house
to which in their trouble
the poor have long been bringing their hymns;
and here the strength surges back to his limbs,
and princely-appareled once more, as in dreams,
he seems
after brief slumber
to rouse
and rise from the rubble
and work his wonder.

97

Der Müde oben tritt tastend ein.
Die Kirche ist schwarz, und das Dunkel ist klein
und wird erst langsam den Blicken weit.
Der Einsame bringt die Ewigkeit
mit in die Mauern und breitet sie aus
mit segnenden Händen—
Da durchweht von den Wänden
lebendige Wärme das Haus.
Und jetzt erst erkennt er: die Kirche log.
Wo der Altar war, da ist neu
eine Krippe gezimmert: Scheu
umdrängen drei Kühe den Trog,
und heufeucht duftet die Streu.
Und die Ewigkeit, die er ausgespannt,
reicht nicht einmal von Wand zu Wand,
wird eine ängstliche Ewigkeit:
denn das Leben ist breit.
Und der Bleiche bleibt einsam an seinem Rand,
bleibt knien.
Und es weht wie aus einer Wiege warm
um ihn.
Und er ist wie ein König aus Morgenland—
nur ganz arm.

98

The weary one gropes his way inside.
The church is black, and the darkness is small
and only slowly is magnified.
The lone one brings with him into the hall
eternity, and spreads it wide
with a holy sign—
live warmth from wall to wall
comes blowing through the shrine.
And now he perceives: the church had lied.
The altar has given way to a stall:
a new-built manger; three timid kine
crowd around the trough;
there's a hay-moist smell from the little straw bed.
And eternity, which he tried to spread
from wall to wall, is not wide enough,
becomes an eternity overawed:
because life is broad.
And the pale one stays alone at the rim,
kneeling.
And as if from a cradle there comes to him
a warm feeling.
And he is like an Orient king of yore—
but quite poor.

DER BLINDE KNABE

An allen Türen blieb der blinde Knabe,
auf den der Mutter bleiche Schönheit schien,
und sang das Lied, das ihm sein Leid verliehn:
"Oh hab mich lieb, weil ich den Himmel habe."
Und alle weinten über ihn.

An allen Türen blieb der blinde Knabe.

Die Mutter aber zog ihn leise mit;
weil sie die andern alle weinen schaute.
Er aber, der nicht wußte, wie sie litt,
und nur noch tiefer seinem Dunkel traute,
sang: "Alles Leben ist in meiner Laute."

Die Mutter aber zog ihn leise mit.

So trug er seine Lieder durch das Land.
Und als ein Greis ihn fragte, was sie deuten,
da schwieg er, und auf seiner Stirne stand:
Es sind die Funken, die die Stürme streuten,
doch einmal werd ich breit sein wie ein Brand.

So trug er seine Lieder durch das Land.

Und allen Kindern kam ein Traurigsein.
Sie mußten immer an den Blinden denken

THE BLIND LAD

At every doorway halted the blind lad
on whom his mother's pallid beauty shone,
and sang the song which grief made his alone:
"Oh love me, because heaven is my own."
And for his sake they all were sad.

At every doorway halted the blind lad.

But mother drew him quietly along,
because they wept for him at every door;
while he, who knew not how much pain she bore,
and trusted in his darkness more and more,
sang: "All of life is leaping in my song."

But mother drew him quietly along.

So through the country with his songs he came.
And when an old man asked him what they meant,
he fell still; but his brow showed their intent:
"These are the sparks which angry storms have sent,
but some day I shall turn into a flame."

So through the country with his songs he came.

And mournfulness caught hold of every child.
The blind one was forever in their thought;

99

und wollten etwas seiner Armut weihn;
er nahm sie lächelnd an den Handgelenken
und sang: "Ich selbst bin kommen euch beschenken."

Und allen Kindern kam ein Traurigsein.

Und alle Mädchen wurden blaß und bang.
Und waren wie die Mutter dieses Knaben,
der immer noch in ihren Nächten sang.
Und fürchteten: wir werden Kinder haben,—
und alle Mütter waren krank . .

    Da wurden ihre Wünsche wie ein Wort
und flatterten wie Schwalben um die Eine,
die mit dem Blinden zog von Ort zu Ort:
"Maria, du Reine,
sieh, wie ich weine.
Und es ist seine
Schuld. In die Haine
führ ihn fort!"

Bei allen Bäumen blieb der blinde Knabe,
auf den der Mutter müde Schönheit schien,
und sang das Lied, das ihm sein Leid verliehn:
"Oh hab mich lieb, weil ich den Himmel habe—"
Und alle blühten über ihm.

100

some gift to ease his poverty they sought;
but, taking each one by the wrist, he smiled:
"I am the gift that unto you is brought."

And mournfulness caught hold of every child.

And pale and frightened all the maidens grew,
much like the mother of this lad who still
was singing through their nights. And not a few
began to tremble: We'll have children, too—
and all the mothers became ill . . .

    Their wishes turned into a word, and flew
like swallows fluttering around the One
who moved from place to place with her blind son:
"Mary, pure of hue,
I weep, see, I do.
And he's to blame. Into
the woods with you
he must be gone!"

At every tree the blind one stopped, on whom
his mother's weatherbeaten beauty shone . . .
and sang the song which grief made his alone:
"Oh love me, because heaven is my own—"
and every tree burst into bloom.

DIE NONNE

Die blonde Schwester trat in ihre Zelle
und schmiegte sich an sie: "Um meine Ruh
ist es geschehn. Ich wurde wie die Welle
und muß den fremden Meeren zu.
Und du bist klar. Du Heilige, du Helle,
mach mich wie du.
Gieb mir den Frieden, den du heimlich hast
und ohne Angst, so wie ihn keine hat,—
gieb mir die Rast;
daß ich ein Fels bin, wenn die Flut mich faßt,
und nicht ein Blatt."

Und leise neigte sich die Nonnenhafte—
nicht tief;
nur wie die Blüte horcht vom hohen Schafte,
wenn Wind sie rief.
Sie hatte längst die Gesten den Geländen
entlernt—die leise gebenden—
und fügte einen Kranz aus ihren Händen
und schenkte lächelnd ihn der Bebenden.

Und nach dem Schweigen waren sie sich nah;
so daß sie sich nicht dunkel fragen mußten
und sich nur klar das Letzte sagen mußten,
und das geschah:

THE NUN

In through the cell-door stepped the fair-haired nun
and knelt to her: "My quietude is gone;
I seem to have become a wave, whipped on
—despite myself—to meet the unknown sea.
And you are pure. You bright, you blessed one,
thus would I be.
Let me possess the peace you have possessed,
and from this terror let me have relief,—
lead me to rest;
that I may be a rock, at the flood's crest,
and not a leaf."

And lightly, slightly, the novitiate bends;
the way
a blossom harks atop its stem, when winds
call it to play.
The worldling's gestures had not come to mind,
not for a long, long while—
and with her hands a garland she entwined
and gave it to the trembler with a smile.

And they felt closer when the silence passed;
their questions need not be mysterious,
and only clear words need be used at last,
and it was thus:

101

"Sprich mir von Christo, dessen Braut du bist,
der dich erkor.
Und seiner Liebe, deren Laut du bist,
tu auf mein Ohr.
Laß mit mich wohnen
in seiner Trauer, deren Trost du bist!
Du Leiserlöste, wie erlost du bist
aus Millionen."

Da küßte kühler sie die Priesterin
und sprach:
"Ich bin ja selbst an Gottes Anbeginn,
und dunkel ist mir meiner Sehnsucht Sinn—
Weit ist der Weg, und keiner weiß wohin,
doch sag ich dir, weil ich die Schwester bin:
Komm nach.
Mit einemmale wird dir Alles weit,
du langst dir nach.
Nur eine Weile geht noch aus der Zeit
die Angst dir nach.
Doch wenn du glaubst, so kann sie weit nicht mit
und sie wird lahm
und bleibt zuletzt.
Und wie es kam?
Das, was ich einmal litt,

"Tell me of Jesus Christ, whose choice you are,
your bridegroom dear,
and breathe his holy love, whose voice you are,
into my ear.
Grant me," she quivered,
"to live within his woe, whose balm you are!
one among millions, safe from harm you are,
gently delivered."

The priestess kissed her in a cooler way:
"My breath
began with God's—I share his natal day,
and I'm not sure what hunger I obey—
the road is long; none guess where it may stray;
but I am Sister to you—so I say:
Come too.
Suddenly all you reach for will grow distant,
vain to pursue.
Fear, beyond Time, for a brief space persistent,
will follow you;
but fear is thwarted if one's faith be true:
it will grow lame
and finally
will stop. And how?
That which once gave me pain

lobpreis' ich jetzt.
Und Nächte giebt es, da die blasse Scham
entflieht,
da schenkt sich Jesus wie ein Lied
mir hin,
und meine Seele sieht,
daß ich ein Wunder bin,
das ihm geschieht.''

Die Schwestern waren Brust an Brust gepreßt
und beide jung im Glühn des gleichen Scheines:

"Dann bin ich mit dem großen Leben Eines
und fühle tief: das ist das Hochzeitsfest,
und all Krüge wurden Krüge Weines."

Da neigten die Mädchen sich Leib an Leib:
es war, als ob derselbe Sturm sie streifte
und sie umwob
und dann die Blonde hob
in einen Sommer hoch, darin sie reifte
—zum Weib.

   Denn sie küßte die Schwester mit fremdem Kuß
und lächelte fremd: "Vergieb,—ich muß.—
Weißt du noch von dem blonden Gespielen?

I worship now.
Some nights my shame flees like a fugitive,
when Christ does give
himself, like a bright melody,
to me,
and then my soul can see
I am a wonder—which
does make him rich."

Breast unto breast the sisters pressed, and each
was young within the flame of the same light:

"Then I am blended with the life divine
and deeply feel: it is the nuptial-rite,
and every jar becomes a jug of wine."

Body to body the girls inclined:
it was as if a single storm had grazed
and intertwined
them, and the blonde one then was raised
to her full height one summer, blooming
—into woman.

   For with a distant kiss she kissed her,
and distantly smiled: "Forgive me, sister,—
I must. —Do you know of my fair-haired friend?

Und wir warfen nach weißen Zielen
schlanke Speere im alten Park:
Der ist jetzt stark."

Und da hielt die Nonne die Schwester nicht—
sah der Schwester nicht ins Gesicht,
ließ sie ganz langsam los,
wurde groß . . .

Die Blonde erschrak; denn kein Segen kam,
und bange bat sie: "So bist du mir gram?"
Die Heilige träumte: Ich hab dich lieb.

Und hielt der Schwester die Hände her,
leer,—
als flehte sie: gieb.

In the old park we used to send
spears against targets when we were young:
now he is strong."

And the nun did not hold the novitiate—
did not look her in the face;
released her slowly from their embrace;
grew great . . .

No blessing the blonde-haired one received,
and in alarm she asked: "Are you peeved?"
"I love you," dreamed the lady of prayer.

And reached her hands toward her sister: bare—
as if
beseeching: give.